PLANETS IN PERIL

PLANETS IN PERIL

A Critical Study of C. S. Lewis's Ransom Trilogy

DAVID C. DOWNING

The University of Massachusetts Press

AMHERST

Printed in the United States of America
LC 91–34369
ISBN 0–87023–997–X
Set in Adobe Garamond by Keystone Typesetting, Inc.
Printed and bound by Thomson-Shore, Inc.

Library of Congress Cataloging-in-Publication Data
Downing, David C.
Planets in peril : a critical study of C.S. Lewis's ransom trilogy
/ David C. Downing
p. cm.
Includes bibliographical references (p.) and index.
ISBN 0–87023–997–X (pbk., alk. paper)
1. Lewis, C.S. (Clive Staples), 1898–1963—Fictional works.
2. Fantastic fiction, English—History and criticism.
3. Christian fiction, English—History and criticism.
4. Theology in literature.
I. Title.
PR6023.E926Z642 1992
823′ .912—dc20 91–34369
CIP

British Library Cataloguing in Publication data are available.

Grateful acknowledgment is made to the following publishers and agencies for permission to quote short excerpts from works by C. S. Lewis:

Cambridge University Press for *The Discarded Images; Selected Literary Essays;* and *Studies in Medieval and Renaissance Literature;* William Collins for *Christian Reflections* © by the Executors of the Estate of C. S. Lewis, 1967, 1980; William B. Eerdmans for *Letters to an American Lady,* ed. Clyde S. Kilby © 1967 by William B. Eerdmans Publishing Company; Harcourt Brace Jovanovich for *Letters of C. S. Lewis* © 1966 by W. H. Lewis and Executors of the Estate of C. S. Lewis; for *Surprised by Joy* © 1955 by C. S. Lewis and renewed by Arthur Owen Barfield, Executor of the Estate of C. S. Lewis; and *The World's Last Night and Other Essays,* © 1958 by C. S. Lewis and renewed 1986 by Arthur Owen Barfield: HarperCollins for *The Abolition of Man: Mere Christianity; Miracles: A Preliminary Study; Out of the Silent Planet; Perelandra; That Hideous Strength;* and *The Weight of Glory and Other Addresses;* Macmillan Publishing for *Letters to Children,* ed. Lyle W. Dorsett and Marjorie Lamp Mead. © 1985 by C. S. Lewis PTE Ltd,; and *They Stand Together: The Letters of C. S. Lewis to Arthur Greaves,* ed. Walter Hooper, © 1979 by C. S. Lewis PTE Ltd.; Oxford University Press for *The Personal Heresy: A Controversy* (1965); *A Preface to Paradise Lost* (1970); and *English Literature in the Sixteenth Century, Excluding Drama* (1954); and to Watkins/Loomis Agency for *Essays Presented to Charles Williams,* first published by Oxford University Press, 1947; paperback edition 1966, published by special arrangement with Florence Sarah Williams.

For Crystal

CONTENTS

ACKNOWLEDGMENTS

My thanks go first to Arthur Lynip, professor emeritus of Westmont College, who introduced me to the Ransom trilogy when I was an undergraduate. Then to Georg Tennyson, professor of English at UCLA, who suggested to me when I was a graduate student that the Ransom trilogy merited a book-length scholarly commentary. After waiting a decade for that commentary to appear, I came to conclude that the task should be mine.

I am grateful to George Blankenbaker, the academic dean at Westmont, for his encouragement and support on this project and for the funds he made available to me to complete my research. Among my faculty colleagues, I wish to thank especially Paul Delaney, professor of English, who I consider the ideal reader for this kind of project. Professors Thomas Schmidt in religious studies and Greg Spencer in communication studies also read portions of the typescript and offered a great deal of useful criticism.

Having taught a summer term course on C. S. Lewis at Westmont College for ten years, I am indebted to the many students who helped sharpen and refine my ideas, noting allusions and motifs I had overlooked and showing the relevance of contemporary critical approaches to the texts produced by Lewis. Among those students who have contributed their insights to this study are Jeremy Kamm, Kara Enroth, Cynthia Ryan, and Craig Berry.

In researching works with such a widespread and diverse readership as the Ransom trilogy, one must necessarily review articles from journals with titles such as *Parma Eldalamberon* or hard-to-find periodicals such as *Cairo Studies in English.* I am indebted to Ned Divelbiss, the associate director of the college library, for his tireless and ingenious work in locating virtually every book and periodical needed.

I wish to express my gratitude to Marie Hass of the Marion C. Wade Collection, Wheaton, Illinois, for her assistance in examining unpublished letters of C. S. Lewis. My thanks go also to my research assistant, Joy Downing Riley, and to Denise Williams Geyer, Marianne Walker, and Stephanie Randolph for additional bibliographic work.

As always, I am deeply grateful to my parents, James and Morena Downing, who gave me a book about C. S. Lewis on my eighteenth birthday with this inscription: "To our son David, who may write books of his own someday."

ABBREVIATIONS OF LEWIS'S WORKS

Note: Throughout the text, quotations from the trilogy are from the 1968 Macmillan edition.

AL	*The Allegory of Love.* London: Oxford UP, 1973. Orig. pub. 1936.
AM	*The Abolition of Man.* New York: Macmillan, 1973. Orig. pub. 1943.
CR	*Christian Reflections.* Grand Rapids, MI: Eerdmans, 1973. Orig. pub. 1967.
DCSL	*All My Road Before Me: The Diary of C. S. Lewis, 1922–1927.* Ed. by Walter Hooper. New York: Harcourt Brace Jovanovich, 1991.
DI	*The Discarded Image.* Cambridge: Cambridge UP, 1971. Orig. pub. 1964.
DT	*The Dark Tower and Other Stories.* Ed. by Walter Hooper. London: Collins; New York: Harcourt Brace Jovanovich, 1977.
EL	*English Literature in the Sixteenth Century, Excluding Drama.* Oxford: Clarendon Press, 1954.
EPCW	*Essays Presented to Charles Williams.* Grand Rapids, MI: Eerdmans, 1977.
FE	*Fern-Seed and Elephants.* New York: Collins/Fountain, 1977. Orig. pub. 1975.
FL	*The Four Loves.* New York: Harcourt Brace Jovanovich, 1960.
GD	*The Great Divorce.* New York: Fontana, 1972. Orig. pub. 1949.
GITD	*God in the Dock.* Grand Rapids, MI: Eerdmans, 1970.
GM	*George Macdonald: An Anthology Edited by C. S. Lewis.* Garden City, NY: Doubleday, 1962.
LAL	*Letters to an American Lady.* Ed. by Clyde S. Kilby. Grand Rapids, MI: Eerdmans, 1967; London: Hodder and Stoughton, 1969.

LCSL	*Letters of C. S. Lewis.* Ed., with a memoir, by W. H. Lewis. London: Geoffrey Bles; New York: Harcourt Brace Jovanovich, 1966.
LTC	*Letters to Children.* Ed. by Lyle W. Dorsett and Marjorie Lamp Meade. New York: Macmillan; London: Collins, 1985.
MC	*Mere Christianity.* New York: Macmillan, 1969. Orig. pub. 1952.
Mir	*Miracles: A Preliminary Study.* New York: Macmillan, 1968. Orig. pub. 1947.
NP	*Narrative Poems.* London: Geoffrey Bles, 1969.
OOW	*Of Other Worlds: Essays and Stories.* New York: Harcourt Brace Jovanovich, 1975.
OS	*On Stories and Other Essays on Literature.* New York: Harcourt Brace Jovanovich, 1982.
OSP	*Out of the Silent Planet.* New York: Macmillan, 1968. Orig. pub. London: John Lane, Bodley Head, 1938; New York: Macmillan, 1943.
Per	*Perelandra.* New York: Macmillan, 1968. Orig. pub. London: John Lane, Bodley Head, 1943; New York: Macmillan, 1944. Also pub. as *Voyage to Venus* (London: Pan Books, 1953).
PH	*The Personal Heresy: A Controversy.* London: Oxford UP, 1965. Orig. pub. 1939.
PP	*The Problem of Pain.* London: Collins, 1972. Orig. pub. 1940.
PPL	*A Preface to Paradise Lost.* London: Oxford UP, 1970. Orig. pub. 1942.
PR	*The Pilgrim's Regress.* New York: Harcourt Brace Jovanovich, 1960. Orig. pub. 1933.
ROE	*Rehabilitations and Other Essays.* London: Oxford UP, 1939.
RP	*Reflections on the Psalms.* New York: Harcourt Brace Jovanovich, 1982. Orig. pub. 1958.
SBJ	*Surprised by Joy.* New York: Harcourt Brace Jovanovich, 1955.
SIL	*Spenser's Images of Life.* Cambridge: Cambridge UP, 1967.
SL	*The Screwtape Letters.* New York: Macmillan, 1960.
SLE	*Selected Literary Essays.* Cambridge: Cambridge UP, 1969.
SMRL	*Studies in Medieval and Renaissance Literature.* Cambridge: Cambridge UP, 1969.
SPT	*Screwtape Proposes a Toast and Other Pieces.* London: Collins, 1971. Orig. pub. 1965.

THS *That Hideous Strength: A Modern Fairy-Tale for Grown-Ups.* New York: Macmillan, 1968. Orig. pub. London: John Lane, Bodley Head, 1945; New York: Macmillan, 1946. Lewis also prepared an abridged version, pub. as *The Tortured Planet* (New York: Avon Books, 1946) and as *That Hideous Strength* (London: Pan Books, 1955).

TST *They Stand Together: The Letters of C. S. Lewis to Arthur Greeves (1914–1963).* Ed. by Walter Hooper. New York: Macmillan; London: Collins, 1979.

WG *The Weight of Glory and Other Addresses.* Grand Rapids, MI: Eerdmans, 1965.

WLN *The World's Last Night and Other Essays.* New York: Harcourt Brace Jovanovich, 1960.

PLANETS IN PERIL

INTRODUCTION

C. S. Lewis (1898–1963) had three careers as a writer, all of them remarkable. He was one of the most distinguished literary critics and scholars of his era, whose works on medieval and Renaissance authors are still considered landmarks in the field. He was also one of the most effective and influential advocates for Christian faith this century. And he produced popular fiction as well, works that continue on best-seller lists a generation after his death. In all, Lewis penned (literally—he never learned to type) nearly forty books in his lifetime, and another ten collections of his essays, lectures, and poems have appeared since his death.

Lewis referred to himself as a living dinosaur, someone largely out of sympathy with the contemporary world (*SLE* 13). Yet worldwide sales of his books have exceeded fifty million copies. Nearly all of Lewis's books remain in print, continuing to sell all together two million copies a year. It is said he detested radio, yet his broadcast talks during World War II made his (after Churchill's) the most recognized voice in Britain.[1]

The life and work of C. S. Lewis abound in such paradoxes. He was unquestionably one of the leading scholars in his discipline, commissioned to write volume 3 (*The Sixteenth Century, Excluding Drama*) for the prestigious *Oxford History of English Literature*. The same year that tome was published (1954), he became professor of medieval and Renaissance English literature at Cambridge, a chair created for him to lure him away from his position at Oxford.[2] This for the man who was fond of declaring that "the Renaissance never happened in England; . . . if it did, it had no importance!"[3]

Lewis is also known as one of the ablest and most cogent defenders of Christianity in this century. Yet he himself did not return to the faith of his childhood until he was almost middle-aged. Even after his reconversion, he confessed that he found Norse and classical mythologies more spontaneously attractive to him than the stories found in the Bible.[4]

Lewis as a writer of fiction is no less enigmatic. He did not marry until his late fifties and had no children of his own. It is generally reported that he was uncomfortable around children. Yet his *Chronicles of Narnia* are acknowledged as classics of children's literature, continuing to sell a million copies a year. His Ransom trilogy was written as "holiday fiction," and he wrote only one handwritten draft of each fantasy, with just a few minor revisions, before sending them off to the publisher.[5] Yet *Out of the Silent Planet, Perelandra,* and *That Hideous Strength* are widely praised for their evident erudition, and even unfavorable reviewers of the trilogy have remarked on the clarity and polish of the author's prose style.

Behind the paradoxes lies a life of extraordinary accomplishment. Lewis was one of only a handful of undergraduates this century to earn three Firsts at Oxford: one in classics, one in ancient philosophy, and one in English literature.[6] His first scholarly book, *The Allegory of Love* (1936), written when he was in his midthirties, was immediately recognized as a major contribution to medieval studies, and it is required reading for graduate students in the field over fifty years later.

As a speaker and teacher, Lewis was unsurpassed. His lectures and sermons at Oxford in the late thirties and forties were delivered to standing-room-only crowds, with members of the audience sitting on the window sills. Dame Helen Gardner has observed that Lewis was "by far the most impressive and exciting person in the faculty of English" at Oxford during the forties.[7] George Bailey adds that it is "almost impossible to exaggerate Lewis's prestige in postwar Oxford." After mentioning other eminent names at Oxford in the field of English letters, Bailey concludes that "they were all, however impressive in themselves, only foothills in the shadow of the towering grandeur of Lewis."[8]

In the mid-1940s Lewis also achieved (unsought) worldwide recognition as a Christian apologist and popular philosopher. His BBC "Broadcast Talks" on Christianity made him a household name in Britain, and his *Screwtape Letters* (1942) became an international best seller. Lewis appeared on the cover of *Time* magazine (8 Sep. 1947).

Given Lewis's formidable reputation as a critic, scholar, and apologist, recognition for his achievement as a fantasy writer has come relatively late. Though his Ransom trilogy was completed in the forties (*Out of the Silent Planet*, 1938; *Perelandra*, 1943; *That Hideous Strength*, 1945) and his *Chronicles of Narnia* in the fifties, there was relatively little scholarly attention during his lifetime to Lewis as fiction writer.

That oversight has been corrected in the past decade. Nearly a dozen books on Lewis's fiction were published in the eighties, and there were a score of dissertations. The Modern Language Association reports that Lewis studies has become one of the most rapidly expanding areas of literary scholarship and interpretation. Apart from a half dozen introductions to Lewis's fiction, there are also five critical studies of the Narnia chronicles available, as well as an excellent book-length analysis of *Till We Have Faces*.[9]

Despite this surge of scholarly interest in the fiction of C. S. Lewis, there is still the need for a sustained analysis of the Ransom trilogy. A spate of introductory overviews of Lewis's fiction as a whole or else topical surveys treat the trilogy in a chapter or two. But the fullness and complexity of this work require more thorough and penetrating analysis. The books of the trilogy continue to fascinate (and, in some cases, infuriate) readers, selling hundreds of thousands of copies each year,[10] even while attracting increased critical attention—as utopian fiction, dystopian fiction, science fiction, and "anti–science fiction."

The books of the trilogy are deceptively simple. All three can be read mainly for the story—*Out of the Silent Planet* as a cosmic voyage, *Perelandra* as an Edenic fantasy, and *That Hideous Strength* as a satire on modern academia. Yet when Lewis became a writer of fantasies, he did not cease to be Lewis the literary critic, Lewis the medieval scholar, or Lewis the Christian apologist and philosopher. Consequently, a full understanding and accurate assessment of the trilogy necessarily rest upon a broader acquaintance with his work—from the poems he wrote in the twenties before his Christian reconversion to posthumous essays not published until the eighties.

An accurate reading of the trilogy must also be based upon an accurate reading of Lewis's life. Though Lewis wrote a memoir of his early years, and though he revealed his personal values in all of his books, his life and mind remain something of a mystery. Even his closest friends reported a certain reticence on his part to speak of anything personal, a habitual veiling of his inner self. Consequently, there remain some basic questions about Lewis the man that cannot help but shape one's interpretations of Lewis the author.

In this book I address these and other issues about C. S. Lewis's life, his worldview, and his literary accomplishment in the trilogy. Chapter 1 offers an outline of Lewis's early life, showing how his reading of his formative years as told in *Surprised by Joy* illuminates many of the central motifs and incidental images of the trilogy. Chapter 2 focuses upon Lewis the Christian apologist, explaining his strategy of "smuggling" theology into readers' minds under the guise of fantasy novels. In chapter 3 it becomes clear just how much Lewis the classical and medieval scholar influenced the work of Lewis the creator of interplanetary fantasies. Chapter 4 surveys the trilogy's portrayal of evil, showing how Lewis drew upon Augustine to explain the nature of evil and upon Dante to show the effects of evil on the human personality. The pilgrim motif is traced throughout the trilogy in chapter 5, recalling Bunyan but also revealing a great deal about Lewis's own spiritual pilgrimage. Chapter 6 explores the complex web of allusions in the trilogy and its chief imaginative and intellectual sources. The concluding chapter provides a broad evaluation and takes up persistent issues raised by reviewers and critics: Was Lewis's lifelong devotion to fantasy a mark of his intellectual independence, or was it a case of arrested emotional development? Were his views on women sexist, even misogynist? How much of his critique of modern science and technology was well informed, and how much was the result of prejudice or habitual suspicion of all things modern? A brief appendix on "The Dark Tower" fragment provides what background is known about this mysterious document, summarizes the story as far as Lewis developed it, and comments on its distinctive Lewisian qualities.

This book is intended to provide the context for an informed reading of the trilogy and to offer a critical assessment of Lewis's literary achievement. I present it as an interpretive guide to *Out of the Silent Planet, Perelandra, That Hideous Strength,* and "The Dark Tower" fragment, as well as a general introduction to one of the most noteworthy minds of our era.

1

"Transfiguring the Past": Lewis's Reading of His Early Life

It is not settled comfort and heart's ease but momentary joy that transfigures the past and lets the eternal quality show through.

C. S. Lewis, unpublished letter, 10 December 1952

IN LEWIS we find a writer of almost bewildering diversity: the medieval historian who wrote letters to children, the literary critic who wrote interplanetary romances, the Christian apologist who composed humorous light verse. Yet one always senses in Lewis's books "the one in the many." His singular way of looking at things, his characteristic habits of thought and speech, developed early in his life and remained remarkably constant. So there is a fascinating interconnectedness in all the books Lewis wrote: reading any one of them casts light upon all the others.

The single most valuable key for interpreting the Ransom trilogy is Lewis's autobiographical memoir *Surprised by Joy: The Shape of My Early Life*. By examining how Lewis shaped his early life experiences into a coherent narrative, readers can best discover how he shaped the theology, the cultural history, and the spiritual autobiography that appear in the trilogy.

At this point readers may wonder if this chapter will be an expression of "the personal heresy," the biographical approach to reading literature that Lewis found so noisome. In his polemical contributions to *The Personal Heresy*, Lewis takes E. M. W. Tillyard,

T. S. Eliot, and others to task for an excessive interest in the mind of the author. Too often, Lewis thought, such an approach distracts readers from the text itself, sometimes even reducing all writing to Freudian confessional, with the author as patient and the critic as analyst.

But Lewis's point in *The Personal Heresy* is not that biographical materials about an author are of no use in helping interpret his or her works. What he objects to, rather, is the relegation of the text to a secondary, or mediary, role in favor of one's primary interest: the "mind" or the "genius" of the author. Lewis insists that texts be studied for the verbal achievements evident on the page, not as "expressions of personality" or as channels for making contact with the writer's soul (1). On the one hand, he objects to "poetolatry"—worship of poets as extraordinary spirits, apart from, and above, ordinary mortals. He argues that the greatness of great writers comes not from their superior souls but from their superior powers of utterance (104–9). On the other hand, Lewis also suspects that many readers want to know all the frank details of authors' lives because they prefer to gossip about great writers rather than to read their books (28).

Yet Lewis did not deny that readers could appreciate more fully the aesthetic effects of imaginative writing by exploring an author's use of imagery in terms of his or her conscious and unconscious mental habits. In his essay "Imagery in the Last Eleven Cantos of Dante's 'Comedy,'" Lewis explains that he intends to examine the image patterns of Dante using a method similar to Caroline Spurgeon's classic study of Shakespeare: "The aim is to surprise the imagination of the poet in its more secret workings, to disengage that incessant orchestration which accompanies his drama and which, though it may escape notice while our attention is fixed on the stage, probably contributes in the highest degree to the total effect" (*SMRL* 78). Lewis adds in the same essay that his principal concern is not to examine the psychology of the author but to understand more fully the aesthetic response of the reader (78–79). These aims, of course, are not mutually exclusive.

Lewis also confessed that the romantic longings he had experienced since early childhood generated their own systems of imagery in his mind and in his books. He labels his pictures of a lost paradise as the "Hesperian or Western Garden system" (*NP* 4), a constellation of images that recurs throughout the books of the trilogy and that predominates in *Perelandra.* The "Hesperian system" is one of many such patterns that make it illuminating to examine Lewis's own life in order to comprehend more fully the key themes and image patterns of the trilogy.

Lewis explains in the preface to *Surprised by Joy* that the book was written to tell how he "passed from Atheism to Christianity," to give an account of his conversion. Some critics, expecting a personal testimony of Lewis's road to faith, are sorely disappointed when they discover that he spends half the book discussing his childhood, boyhood, and adolescence, spending only a few pages recounting his actual conversion experience in his early thirties. For example, one of Lewis's more meticulous readers, John Beversluis, looks for a philosophical defense of faith in *Surprised by Joy* and registers his dissatisfaction: "The book abounds with tangents and asides: [Lewis] denounces English boarding schools; . . . he criticizes many of the social conventions that had been imposed on him as a child; he bristles about games and other forms of enforced recreation that he says deprive children of their individuality; he airs many of his well-known pet peeves about modern life. In short *Surprised by Joy* is a very mixed bag."[1]

Given Lewis's own statements in the preface about telling the story of his conversion, the disappointment of some readers is understandable. However, Lewis also states in the preface that *Surprised by Joy* is "suffocatingly subjective" (viii) and that readers may discover after only a few pages that it is not what they were hoping for. Surely enough, the first page of the text explores the differing temperaments Lewis saw in his father's side of the family and his mother's. The subject is personal origins, not philosophical starting points. The tone is one of meditation and reverie, not of apologetics or testimony.

The Lewis of *Surprised by Joy,* published in 1955, is not quite the same Lewis who had sallied forth so brilliantly, and so controversially, to defend his Christian worldview in a seemingly endless stream of books, essays, and debates in the thirties and forties. The same year *Surprised by Joy* was published, Lewis wrote to the Milton Society of America, commenting on the central impulse behind all his books.

> The list of my books which I send . . . will I fear strike you as a very mixed bag . . . (but) there is a guiding thread. The imaginative man in me is older, more continuously operative, and in that sense more basic than either the religious writer or the critic. It was he who made me first attempt (with little success) to be a poet. It was he who, in response to the poetry of others, made me a critic, and, in defence of that response, sometimes a critical controversialist. It was he who after my conversion led me to embody my religious belief in symbolical or mythopoeic forms, ranging from *Screwtape* to a kind of theologised science fiction. And it was of course he who has brought me, in the last few years, to write the series of Narnian stories for children. (*LCSL* 260)

Here in Lewis's own synopsis of his life as a writer we find the "guiding thread" for understanding his purposes in *Surprised by Joy*. He shapes his memories of his early years in order to explore the roots of his imaginative and intellectual life, to trace "the growth of the poet's mind." *Surprised by Joy* should be read less in the spirit of Newman's *Apologia pro Vita Sua* than in the spirit of Wordsworth's *Prelude*, one of the poems Lewis said he turned to more than any other. In fact Lewis himself invites us to make the comparison in the first chapter of *Surprised by Joy*, stating that he wants to record his imaginative experiences in the tradition of Traherne and Wordsworth (*SBJ* 16). Even the title, *Surprised by Joy*, is from a well-known Wordsworth sonnet.

Lewis's own version of emotions recollected in tranquillity is built upon a number of interwoven motifs. Lewis, who confesses to being a romantic early on in the autobiography (5), does just what we would expect a romantic to do: he structures his biography not linearly but symphonically, finding an organic form in those early years. What Beversluis calls a "mixed bag" is better seen as an intricate tapestry of remembrance and reflection. Another Lewis scholar, reading *Surprised by Joy* for its art rather than for its philosophy, has pronounced it "arguably . . . the best autobiography of the twentieth century."[2]

As mentioned above, Lewis begins *Surprised by Joy* with a dramatic contrast, relating the differing temperaments of his father and mother to their family histories. He calls his father's people "true Welshmen, sentimental, passionate, and rhetorical, easily moved both to anger and to tenderness; men who laughed and cried a great deal and who had not much of the talent for happiness." In contrast, Lewis's mother's family, the Hamiltons, were "a cooler race" whose minds were "critical and ironic" and who possessed a "talent for happiness in a high degree" (*SBJ* 3). George Sayer, Lewis's best biographer and clearly a great admirer of Lewis, gently corrects his former mentor on this account, pointing out that Lewis's maternal grandfather, a minister, was an extremely emotional man, given to weeping from the pulpit and to accusing Roman Catholics of consorting with the devil. Sayer adds that Lewis's description of the Hamiltons (5) does not fit even his mother herself.

Lewis's somewhat inaccurate recollection of his mother and her family may reveal more about him than if his portrait of her had been scrupulously factual. It suggests that what his mother stood for—"coolness," temperate emotion—was more real to him than the kind of literal facts that might be unearthed by a biographer. Coolness for Lewis was nearly always a term of approbation, connoting mildness, freshness, freedom from tyrannical passions. The contrast between his father and mother in the opening pages of *Surprised by Joy* also reveals Lewis's image of himself as a fusion of opposites, a walking embodiment of Hegelian synthesis.

Lewis habitually interpreted ideas and experiences dualistically. In his apologetic books, he frequently brings readers to a crossroads, an either-or situation. Then he shows why one choice simply will not do and invites us to travel down the other road a while. Soon we face another crossroads, with one of the choices again disappointing, and so on, until soon it seems that there is no other sensible point of view than the one Lewis has been leading to. This technique delights some readers, who find in Lewis a path through the wilderness, a route through the intellectual maze of twentieth-century thought. Others, however, react with annoyance, complaining loudly about oversimplification, about reducing opponents to straw figures, calling Lewis a "pious paradox-monger and audacious word juggler."[3]

Lewis's dialectical habit of mind is equally evident in *Surprised by Joy*, but there is a difference. In interpreting his own life, Lewis again finds a series of dynamic oppositions: childhood vs. boyhood, intellect vs. imagination, belief vs. skepticism. Here, however, we do not find simple either-or alternatives. Rather, Lewis presents his life as a series of antitheses that forced him to develop a strategy for some higher synthesis. These dialectical subtexts provide the organic structure of *Surprised by Joy*. They also provide an interpretive frame for some of the dominant image patterns of the Ransom trilogy.

Childhood vs. Boyhood

Ruth Pitter, one of Lewis's closest female friends during his forties and fifties, observed that his reaction to life reflected "an almost uniquely persisting *child's* sense of glory and nightmare."[4] At first glance, this hardly seems a likely description of the author of the massively erudite *Allegory of Love*, of the brashly polemical sections of *A Personal Heresy*, and of the wittily "diabolic" *Screwtape Letters*. Yet Pitter's observation is corroborated by many others who knew Lewis. It helps explain many of the surprising features of Lewis's fiction, and it also illuminates Lewis's reading of his own early life.

In *Surprised by Joy* Lewis presents his early years as a nearly idyllic "childhood" at home followed by a traumatic "boyhood" in the public schools. These are synthesized finally in adult life with Lewis's recovery of faith and discovery of his true vocation. (Though Lewis never showed a great deal of interest in Blake, his categories of development certainly recall Blake's stages of innocence, experience, and "organized innocence.")

Critics and biographers generally speak of Lewis's early years using the terms *childhood* and *boyhood* interchangeably. This usage overlooks the more precise meaning that Lewis lent to each term. *Child* and *boy* have consistent, and contrasting, connotations, not only in *Surprised by Joy,* but in all of Lewis's writings. (For Lewis, seemingly general terms often took on specific personal meanings, which he consistently applied in a variety of contexts. Those who read widely in Lewis, for example, will discover that general terms such as *joy, comfort, taste,* and *pagan* have special, technical meanings in the Lewis lexicon.)

For Lewis, *childhood* referred to the years from his birth (in Belfast in 1898) until he was nine, the year his mother died and he was sent off to boarding school in England. These were years of some nightmares, but mostly of glory, that held almost mythic status in the mind of the adult Lewis. The subtitle of the first chapter is taken from Milton's description of Adam and Eve in prelapsarian Eden: "Happy, but for so happy ill secured" (*Paradise Lost,* 4, 370).

Lewis remembers his childhood for "good parents, good food, and a garden . . . to play in," as well as two other blessings—his nurse, Lizzie Endicott, and his brother, Warren, three years older (*SBJ* 5). He describes Lizzie with more nostalgia and affection than he does his own mother, saying that "even the exacting memory of childhood can discover no flaw—nothing but kindness, gaiety, and good sense," concluding that she was "as nearly as a human can be, simply good" (5). Though hardly more than a thumbnail sketch, Lewis's fond recollection of his childhood nurse illustrates how *Surprised by Joy* can function as a key to his personal mythology. Throughout the diverse books of the Lewis oeuvre, the words *nurse* and *nursery* virtually always connote that which is simple, but also that which is true and good. For example, he warns in his essay "The Poison of Subjectivism": "Unless we return to the crude and nursery-like belief in objective values, we perish" (*CR* 81). In *That Hideous Strength* one of the women at St. Anne's reminds Jane Studdock of her childhood nurse (30); in contrast, when her husband, Mark, tries to get a straight answer from one of the leaders at N.I.C.E., the other answers testily that he is not Mark's nurse (111).

From the metaphors alone, experienced readers of Lewis can tell which of the two Studdocks is keeping the right company.

The other blessing mentioned by Lewis—his brother, Warren—was a lifelong companion and one who helped shape the way in which Lewis defined himself in relation to the world. "Warnie" and "Jack" (as Clive dubbed himself at the age of three) spent many a rainy afternoon poring over the books in their parents' well-stocked library, delighting especially in E. Nesbit, Beatrix Potter, and stories of "knights-in-armour," as well as "dressed animals" (*SBJ* 14–15). They also created their own imaginary worlds of "India" and "Animal-Land," later combined into the kingdom of Boxen. Though the worlds they created seemed prosaic to Lewis as an adult, they show how much time the two spent together, content in each other's company, and trying to keep as free as possible from adult interference.

Lewis does discuss one upsetting element in those early years, but the source came from within, not without. He had particularly acute childhood fears of specters and insects, recalling especially a frightful picture of a midget child threatened by a stag beetle with movable horns like pincers (*SBJ* 9). These childhood bogies—specters, insects, especially beetles—reappear in Lewis's fiction, illustrating how imaginative creation could be for him an opportunity for what D. H. Lawrence called "shedding one's sicknesses in books."

In general, Lewis recalls his childhood years before his mother's death in terms of a happy and secure home, the simple goodness of a beloved nurse, and the freedom to roam through empires of imagination with his brother, Warren. And the words *child* and *childhood,* sometimes even *childish,* tend to carry the same connotations in all of Lewis's books—simplicity, self-forgetfulness, imagination, and wonder. For example, in *Out of the Silent Planet,* Ransom's first look at the beautiful landscape of another world reminds him of a child's watercolor painting (42). In *Perelandra* Ransom answers Weston's self-absorbed jabbering about his fear of death by telling him to say a child's prayer (171).

But Lewis's childhood came to an abrupt end when his mother died. Besides losing his mother, Jack in a very real sense lost his father and his home as well. He reports that his father, Albert Lewis, always a highly emotional man, became increasingly subject to fits of temper after his wife's death, responding to his sons unpredictably and sometimes unjustly. This drew the two brothers even closer together, "two frightened urchins huddled for warmth in a bleak world" (*SBJ* 19).

Lewis dwells at some length on his mother's death, but he emphasizes not the intensity of his bereavement so much as other traumas that complicated his grief. Apart from increasing estrangement from his father, he recalls having to view his mother's body as an ordeal when "grief was overwhelmed in terror." He adds that "the ugliest man alive is an angel of beauty compared with the loveliest of the dead" (*SBJ* 20). Lewis remembers as well that he "reacted with horror" at all the fuss and flummery of the funeral, confessing a lifelong distaste for the public, the collective, and an inaptitude for formality. Clearly, his mother's death and funeral were searing events for the young Lewis, events that he could describe vividly and affectingly nearly fifty years later. The images and emotional intensity found in these pages of *Surprised by Joy* recur, sometimes in disguised form, in all three books of the Ransom trilogy.

Not long after his mother's death, Jack, not yet ten, was sent off to England to begin his formal education, a custom still not uncommon among the well-to-do in Ireland. He joined his brother at a school in Hertfordshire called Wynyard, one Lewis called Belsen, after the Nazi concentration camp. He was abjectly miserable there, and for good reason. "Oldie," their schoolmaster, was an arbitrary and sadistic man, whose frequent rages were accompanied by canings and severe verbal abuse. The conditions at the school—a lack of hot meals, of sanitation, or of any concern for genuine learning—sound like something out of Dickens. Readers have wondered if Lewis does not exaggerate the privations and the brutality of life at Wynyard, but his memories are confirmed by his brother, Warren, and by other unfortunates who attended the school at the same time as the Lewis brothers.[5] In fact, the school closed down two years after Jack came there, and Oldie was later certified as insane.[6] A few months before his death in 1963, Lewis wrote that, after half a century of effort, he had finally forgiven the man who had so scarred his earliest boyhood.[7]

First united against their increasingly mercurial father and then united against a pitiless schoolmaster, Warren and Jack learned to depend on each other for support. Lewis comments that this pattern, occurring twice so early in his life, permanently affected his whole outlook: "To this day the vision of the world which comes most naturally to me is one in which 'we two' or 'we few' (and in a sense 'we happy few') stand together against something stronger and larger" (*SBJ* 32). The references to "we few" and "we happy few" come from *Henry V*, and the context is revealing. There Henry exhorts his earls to take heart, even though they go into battle outnumbered five to one by the French. He tells them to fight for honor's sake, and for their comrades' sake, concluding that, whether in victory or defeat, the world would remember "we few, we happy few, we band of brothers" (4, 3, 60).

Wynyard set the tone for Lewis's experience in boarding schools. After Wynyard "sank unlamented," Lewis spent a brief stint at Campbell College, only a mile from his boyhood home in Belfast. Though he did not stay at Campbell long enough to develop vivid impressions, his narrative underscores the feelings of rootlessness that plagued his school years. "From my point of view the great drawback was that one had, so to speak, no home. Only a few very senior boys had studies. The rest of us, except when seated at table for meals or in a huge 'preparation room' for evening 'Prep,' belonged nowhere. . . . One was always 'moving on' or 'hanging about'—in lavatories, in store rooms, in the great hall. It was very like living permanently in a large railway station" (*SBJ* 51).

Lewis left Campbell because of ill health, and the following term, at the age of twelve, he went to "Chartres" (actually Cherbourg House), a prep school for Malvern College. Though certainly happier there than he had been at Wynyard, Lewis continues to portray his school as a retrogression from childhood years. He reports that at Cherbourg House he lost what childhood faith he had had and learned affectation and vulgarity from their worldly young master, whom Lewis calls Pogo. "What attacked me through Pogo was not the Flesh (I had that of my own) but the World: the desire for glitter, swagger, distinction, the desire to be in the know. He . . . made sad work of certain humble and childlike and self-forgetful qualities which (I think) had remained with me till that moment. I began to labour very hard to make myself into a fop, a cad, and a snob" (*SBJ* 68).

Even though he was acquiring mannerisms he would later disdain, Jack was fairly happy at Cherbourg. One can almost measure Lewis's emotional response to the schools he attended by the degree to which they simulated a home environment. His relative contentment at Cherbourg House is clearly linked to the matron there, who acted as a surrogate mother for the boys. Lewis describes her with the same unabashed affection he had expressed in his earlier depiction of his childhood nurse. He concludes his portrait of the matron at Cherbourg House with a revelatory summation, "We all loved her; I, the orphan, especially" (*SBJ* 59).

After two years at Cherbourg House came Malvern College, where Lewis became again intensely unhappy. The regimentation and the required games there were a trial for Lewis, but even more he despised the social hierarchy in which the in-group, or "Bloods," most often athletes, were accorded privilege and prestige, and before whom the others were supposed to grovel. At first, his situation at Malvern seemed "the bare 'I' against what simply seemed the world" (*SBJ* 104). But once he found a few friends who shared his literary tastes, he again had a sense of "we few" so that *the* world of the Bloods became only *a* world, a world of "Games and Gallantry" that he need not submit to. As he grew older, Lewis became accustomed to this stance and even began to revel in it. He says that England's perilous stand in 1940 before a seemingly invincible Germany felt familiar to him (*SBJ* 32). He later relished his role as torchbearer for "we few" against the armies of progressivism, collectivism, and modernism in general.

At that age, however, Lewis was not ready to take on the world.

He wrote repeatedly to his father asking to be removed from Malvern, eventually threatening to shoot himself unless his father would allow him to withdraw.[8] Accordingly, Albert Lewis sent him to live with a private tutor named William Kirkpatrick, who ran a small "cramming school" in Great Bookham, Surrey. "Kirk," or the "Great Knock" (as he was dubbed by the Lewis family), had been the schoolmaster at Lurgan College, which Albert had attended, and for whom he had a great deal of admiration and fond, if sentimental, memories.

Kirkpatrick turned out to be utterly unlike Albert's maudlin reminiscences. He was a forthright and skeptical man, an atheist of the old-fashioned Thomas Huxley variety. Lewis says he "came near to being a purely logical entity," who considered even the most casual remark as a "summons to disputation" (*SBJ* 136). Many a fourteen-year-old would have quavered under such a teacher, but the young Lewis thrived under his tutelage as "red beef and strong beer" (136). Under Kirkpatrick, Lewis read Greek and Latin authors in the original languages, mastered French and Italian, and studied German. He saved for "leisure reading" British authors whom American students usually do not study until graduate school. Kirkpatrick reappears in the form of MacPhee, a canny Irishman in "The Dark Tower" and *That Hideous Strength.*

Lewis's biographers agree that the two and a half years that Jack spent at Great Bookham were the most peaceful of his entire life.[9] There Lewis escaped the collective regimen of the public schools and recovered a homelike environment. He reports that the country houses he saw when he first arrived in Surrey answered to his idea of happiness and filled him for a desire for "domesticity" that he had never fully known (*SBJ* 132–33). Under Kirkpatrick began a healing process that was not completed until Lewis fully reclaimed his childhood in his early thirties.

After Great Bookham came University College, Oxford. Lewis still referred to himself as a boy when he arrived at Oxford, one "nearly without a moral conscience" (*PP* 26.) Despite the halcyon days under his beloved Kirk, Lewis had also a long way yet to go in his search for a vision of reality that was logically defensible as well as emotionally satisfying. The flippant skepticism of his public school years was reinforced by Kirkpatrick's more rigorous variety. And the seventeen-year-old Lewis was still tainted by the traumas of Wynyard, the rootlessness of Campbell, and the false sophistication of Cherbourg House and Malvern.

The contrast between childhood and boyhood recurs throughout *Surprised by Joy.* When describing his first set of schoolclothes, he recalls wistfully the freedom and comfort of a child's playwear and then comments on the misery of his new uniform: "Now I am choking and sweating, itching too, in thick dark stuff, throttled by an Eton collar, my feet already aching with unaccustomed boots. . . . Worst of all is the bowler-hat, apparently made of iron, which grasps my head" (*SBJ* 22). A few pages later Lewis remembers with pleasure the conversation of his fellow sufferers at Wynyard, whose talk "was not bound down to the narrow interests which satisfy public school boys" because they "still had the curiosity of children" (*SBJ* 32).

The most resounding critique of the values of boyhood comes in a key passage where Lewis describes the beginnings of his emergence from that regrettable state. He depicts adolescence, the twilight of boyhood, as a kind of Renaissance.

> For boyhood is very like the "dark ages" not as they were but as they are represented in bad, short histories. The dreams of childhood and those of adolescence may have much in common; between them, often, boyhood stretches like an alien territory in which everything (ourselves included) has been greedy, cruel, noisy, and prosaic, in which the imagination has slept and the most unideal senses and ambitions have been relentlessly, even maniacally, awake.
>
> In my own life it was certainly so. My childhood is at unity with the rest of my life; my boyhood not so. (*SBJ* 71–72)

For Lewis, the child was truly the father to the man. That intervening state, boyhood, is referred to censoriously wherever it appears in Lewis's books. When in "*De Futilitate*" he calls materialism "a philosophy for boys" (*CR* 71), he is speaking pejoratively but also autobiographically: materialism was the philosophy that had dominated his own boyhood years. Note similar connotations in the essay "Shelley, Dryden, and Mr Eliot," where he critiques the pose of "disillusionment."

> Men (and, still more, boys) like to call themselves disillusioned because the very form of the word suggests that they have had the illusions and emerged from them—have tried both worlds. The claim, however, is false in nine cases out of ten. The world is full of impostors who claim to be disenchanted and are really unenchanted: mere "natural" men who have never risen so high as to be in danger of the generous illusions they claim to have escaped from. . . . They talk like sages who have passed through the half-truths of humanitarian benevolence, aristocratic honour, or romantic passion, while in fact they are clods who have never yet advanced so far. (*SLE* 196)

References to boyhood in the Ransom stories carry the same connotations. When Weston reveals in "a schoolboy's whisper" that he has discovered a force in the universe (*Per* 92), the metaphor provides an early hint of the sort of force he has discovered. And when Knellie is introduced in "The Dark Tower" as someone Lewis knew in school (29), the narrative implies that Knellie is not someone Lewis is glad to know as an adult.

Though Lewis considered himself a boy when he first came to Oxford, his arrival there marked the beginning of what now would be called a major "paradigm shift." His first experience in the renowned city was a comical one but also, he felt, a deeply significant one. He reports that he came out of the railway station, loaded down with luggage, and headed down the street in the wrong direction, away from the colleges. He kept walking, increasingly disappointed by the uncomely houses and shops he saw, until he came near to the edge of the city: "Only when it became obvious that there was very little town left ahead of me, that I was in fact getting to open country, did I turn round and look. There, behind me, far away, never more beautiful since, was the fabled cluster of spires and towers. I had come out of the station on the wrong side and been all this time walking into what was even then the mean and sprawling suburb of Botley. I did not see to what extent this little adventure was an allegory of my whole life" (*SBJ* 184).

Lewis read this incident as an allegory of his whole life because it showed that for too long he had been walking in the wrong direction. For him boyhood had been a kind of "fall" from childhood. For him becoming a "grown-up" would be a further step in the wrong direction. Throughout the autobiography, as well as in Lewis's fiction, *grown-up* usually connotes a state of dreary practicality, in which utility and "getting ahead" predominate, or where the sneerings and snobberies of boyhood take on even more sinister manifestations (see, for example, *SBJ* 43, 48).[10] For him, the path less taken involved a return to childhood, to a sense of wonder, glory, even nightmare, instead of submitting to the mundanities and inanities he found all too prevalent in modern life.

Not surprisingly, Lewis's books abound in metaphors of return, of looking back or going back. In the highly autobiographical *Pilgrim's Regress,* John, the protagonist, finds himself by going full circle and discovering the true meaning of his starting point as a child. In *The Great Divorce* Lewis answers Blake's "Marriage of Heaven and Hell" by saying that good comes only by undoing evil, not by trying to wed the two: "I do not think that all who choose wrong roads perish; but their rescue consists in being put back on the right road. A wrong sum can be put right: but only by going back till you find the error and working it afresh from that point, never by simply *going on.* Evil can be undone, but it cannot 'develop' into good. Time does not heal it" (*GD* 6).

Here Lewis is speaking primarily of ethics. As can be seen, he did not believe that if we walk far enough in the wrong direction, we will eventually find ourselves somehow back on the right path. (This is where he would disagree with Hegel, as well as Blake.) Rather one must simply turn and go back—to recover what has been lost, to reclaim "the truth in old books," sometimes even to repent. Lewis uses a similar strategy in *Miracles,* where the subject is metaphysics: "Only Supernaturalists really see Nature. You must go a little away from her, and then turn round, and look back. Then at last the true landscape will become visible. You must have tasted, however briefly, the pure water from beyond the world before you can be distinctly conscious of the hot, salty tang of Nature's current.

To treat her as God, or as Everything, is to lose the whole pith and pleasure of her. Come out, look back, and then you will see" (*Mir* 67).

The idea of return meant more to Lewis than just a recovery of childhood. For him the need to look back, or to go back, took many forms: a return to the classics and to neglected authors, to objective moral values, to a traditional Christian understanding of the universe and our place in it. The strategy of moving forward by going back is also a key to the resolution of two other tensions that dominated Lewis's early years: imagination vs. intellect and belief vs. skepticism.

Imagination vs. Intellect

George Sayer has remarked on Lewis's uncanny ability to "recall and live imaginatively in the world of childhood."[11] This is true in one sense and not true in another. For *Surprised by Joy* offers few external details about the world of Ulster at the turn of the century. On the one hand, we see very little of Belfast or the countryside (except for the Castlereagh hills, to which the Lewis brothers attached a special meaning). We hear very little about visits to the seaside, which Jack and Warnie reveled in, and even a family trip to the coast of Normandy evokes no impressions worth recording. On the other hand, Lewis can recall vividly specific lines he read in books or the pictures used to illustrate them. Lewis truly does capture the selective attention of a child, especially a precocious child of a literary nature. He also gives us little reason to doubt his assertion that "at the age of six, seven, and eight, I was living almost entirely in my imagination" (*SBJ* 15).

The most intense and significant imaginative experiences of Lewis's childhood are the recurrences of "Joy," his word for *Sehnsucht,* the longing for some lost paradise that is itself a kind of paradise to feel. Lewis recalls one summer day when he was only six that there arose in him a memory "as if from a depth not of years but of centuries" of an earlier time when his brother had brought a toy garden into the nursery. Lewis compares the momentary sensation that came with the memory to Milton's "enormous bliss" of Eden. The experience left a permanent imprint on his imagination: "That was the first beauty I ever knew. What the real garden had failed to do, the toy garden did. It made me aware of nature . . . as something cool, dewy, fresh, exuberant. . . . As long as I live my imagination of Paradise will retain something of my brother's toy garden" (*SBJ* 7).

Even as a child, though, Lewis recognized that the feeling evoked by the memory was not a desire for a handful of moss arranged on a biscuit tin, not even for his own past. A desire then for what? Trying to answer that question became a kind of personal grail quest for Jack, one that would lead toward many false objects of desire—eroticism, the occult, worldly success—until he finally found what he considered to be the true object of Joy, or "Sweet Desire."

Later, in reading Beatrix Potter's *Squirrel Nutkin,* and again when reading Longfellow's translations of Icelandic saga, the young Lewis again experienced a nameless longing, an "unsatisfied desire which is itself more desirable than any other satisfaction" (*SBJ* 17–18). Through the first of these came the "Idea of Autumn" (16), refracted through the homeliness of animals who behave like sturdy English yeomen. Through the second came Lewis's first introduction to "Northernness," a stern and ecstatic vision of things "cold, spacious, severe, pale, and remote" (17).

Lewis reports that when he was sent off to school, his experiences of Joy ceased for a time, and his imaginative life in general suffered. His explanation for this is certainly in keeping with his reading of childhood and boyhood: "When the boy passes from nursery literature to school-stories he is going down, not up. *Peter Rabbit* pleases a disinterested imagination, for the child does not want to be a rabbit, though he may like pretending to be a rabbit as he may later like acting Hamlet; but the story of the unpromising boy who became captain of the First Eleven exists precisely to feed his real ambitions" (*SBJ* 35).

Though Lewis was reading Greek and Roman authors at school, and dipped into Rider Haggard, H. G. Wells, and even John Milton for his own pleasure, he holds his imaginative life during his boyhood years of little account, a time almost bereft of Sweet Desire. Finally, the "dark ages" of boyhood began to recede when he rediscovered "Northernness," one of the forms of Joy that he had experienced while reading Icelandic saga as a child. Casually glancing at the cover of a literary magazine someone had left lying in a classroom, his eyes encountered the phrase *Siegfried and the Twilight of the Gods,* accompanied by an Arthur Rackham illustration. All at once, he was engulfed in a "vision of huge, clear spaces hanging above the Atlantic in the endless twilight of Northern summer," a vision that made him feel that, after an absence of several years, he was "returning at last from exile and desert lands" to his own country (*SBJ* 73). From that time on, Lewis read with religious devotion everything he could on Norse mythology, with feelings of love and awe that his earlier Christian beliefs had never elicited.

Like Warnie's make-believe garden, "Northernness" was a catalyst of Joy that Lewis would make use of in his own fiction. *Out of the Silent Planet,* particularly, contains a great deal of "Northernness." The pale blue sky and bracing atmosphere of Malacandra remind us that Lewis's favorite season was winter. The Malacandrian words *hross, handramit,* and *harandra* are derived from Old Norse words for *horse, lowlands,* and *highlands,* respectively.[12] Even incidental references in *Out of the Silent Planet* to Rackham (112) and Chaliapin, the Russian operatic singer (155), evoke "Northernness," alluding to Norse saga as portrayed in the illustrations of Rackham or performed in Wagnerian operas.

Lewis reports that he lived in two worlds during his last few years at school: on the outside, living the life of a typical English schoolboy; on the inside, a quester after Joy, reading about Teutonic myth, listening to Wagner, looking at the illustrations of Rackham. This dualism continued during Jack's remaining years in school, broadening into a general opposition between intellect and imagination. He discovered that the things he considered good and those he considered real were almost mutually exclusive: "Such then was the state of my imaginative life; over against it stood the life of my intellect. The two hemispheres of my mind were in sharpest contrast. On the one side a many-islanded sea of poetry and myth; on the other a glib and shallow 'rationalism.' Nearly all that I loved I believed to be imaginary; nearly all that I believed to be real I thought grim and meaningless" (*SBJ* 170).

Here Lewis stacks the cards a bit in referring to his "glib and shallow 'rationalism.'" But through most of his teens and twenties the cards were stacked in the other direction. The things that evoked Joy—mythology, romance, fairy tale—were things his intellect scorned. At one point, under the influence of Freud and others, he dismissed his unattainable hills, his paradisal gardens, and other images of desire as wish-fulfillment fantasies: "With the confidence of a boy I decided I had done with all that. No more Avalon, no more Hesperides. I had . . . 'seen through' them. And I was never going to be taken in again" (*SBJ* 204).

But the reality his intellect presented to him was hardly a substitute. He envisioned nothing but an empty cosmos with no spiritual beings in it except some accidental creatures on a spinning speck of dust, creatures whose history was mainly one of suffering, cruelty, and war—with death and absurdity always the victors. (Those who think Lewis never grasped the force of atheism or knew what despair felt like need only read the opening pages of *The Problem of Pain.*)

As can be seen, the need to reconcile intellect and imagination became more and more intertwined with the problem of developing a worldview that would be satisfying to both sides of Lewis's bifurcated personality. On the one hand, his imagination, especially his glimpses of Joy, seemed to suggest some hidden glory at the center of things. On the other hand, his intellect pointed in exactly the opposite direction.

Lewis did reconcile the two, or at least he found a strategy to avoid a kind of lifelong metaphysical schizophrenia. But the resolution to this quandary is closely bound up with another major tension of his early years: belief vs. skepticism. For him, a single stroke untangled not one Gordian knot but two. Accordingly, we must examine this third major dualism before discussing how Lewis emerged with a coherent worldview that fused imagination and intellect and that launched him on one of the most extraordinary writing careers of the twentieth century.

Belief vs. Skepticism

Given Lewis's aversion for so much of what occurred during his school years, one might suppose that he would associate simple Christian faith with his childhood, loss of faith with his boyhood, and recovery of faith with emergence from boyhood. But as Lewis would say, reality has its ragged edges, and so the story of his spiritual journey is not that symmetrical.

Some readers of Lewis have linked his vigorous convictions with his Ulster Protestant background, assuming that his upbringing must have been tinged by a sharp puritanical hue. But Lewis corrects the record on this account, reporting that his father preferred High Church forms of worship and that he could remember nothing of his mother's religion (*SBJ* 8, 34). Neither did his mother's death elicit any true religious feeling, according to Lewis. During her illness he prayed for her recovery, and when she died, he prayed that she could be miraculously returned to life. But Lewis explains that the failure of his prayers did not produce a loss of belief in him because there was no genuine belief there in the first place: "I think the truth is that the belief into which I had hypnotised myself was itself too irreligious for its failure to cause any religious revolution. I had approached God, or my idea of God, without love, without awe, even without fear. He was, in my mental picture of this miracle, to appear neither as Saviour nor as Judge, but merely as a magician; and when He had done what was required of Him I supposed He would simply—well, go away" (*SBJ* 21).

Lewis mentions several times his constitutional dislike of being imposed upon or interfered with (*SBJ* 47). It is clear that his earliest conception of God as "genie in a bottle" is influenced by this feeling. The problem of surrendering, of affirming a God with every right to "interfere," was the last great obstacle Lewis had to overcome before his final conversion more than two decades after his mother's death. This same trait marks Ransom in *Out of the Silent*

Planet, "Lewis" in *Perelandra,* and Jane Studdock in *That Hideous Strength.*

Lewis writes that his first authentic belief came at Wynyard, the wretched boarding school he was sent to after his mother's death. Attending Anglo-Catholic services twice a week, he heard all the doctrines of the Christian faith expounded by people who clearly believed in them and considered them vital. Unfortunately, his newfound beliefs did not provide him assurance or comfort but rather served to compound his fears. Lewis vividly recalls lying awake fearing for his soul on "certain blazing moonlit nights in that curtainless dormitory" at Wynyard (*SBJ* 34). The image of moonlight streaming in on sleepless nights occurs three more times in *Surprised by Joy,* always with connotations of boyhood fears. So when a similar image appears in *Out of the Silent Planet,* we have some confidence about its significance for Lewis.

Jack lost this early, harrowing faith at the age of twelve or thirteen while he was at Cherbourg House. The matron there, the one who served as a kind of foster mother, conveyed to the young Lewis, not intentionally, a sense that Christianity was only one belief system among many, and certainly not the most compelling. Understandably, Lewis describes the loss of his earlier convictions as the casting off of a great burden: "And oh, the relief of it! Those moonlit nights in the dormitory at Belsen faded far away. From the tyrannous noon of revelation I passed into the cool evening of Higher Thought, where nothing was to be obeyed, and nothing to be believed except what was either comforting or exciting" (*SBJ* 60). This passage supports one of Lewis's arguments that appears in several of his books: one cannot dismiss religious belief as simple wish fulfillment because unbelief may often fulfill one's wishes better than belief.

The glib freethinking of Lewis's years at Cherbourg House and Malvern found a firmer foundation when he went to study with Kirkpatrick. There, steeped in Schopenhauer and in comparative religion, he became quite an articulate agnostic, as can be seen in his letters to his boyhood friend Arthur Greeves. (See *TST* 134–35, for example.)

But one's reading can subvert skepticism as well as belief. For

Lewis the first jolt came when he read George Macdonald's *Phantastes.* He found a "cool morning innocence" (*GM* 26) in the book, and he found the romance he already loved in Spenser, Malory, and Yeats combined with a new quality: holiness. Lewis recalls that in reading Macdonald, "for the first time the song of the sirens sounded like the voice of my mother or my nurse" (*SBJ* 179). This last phrase implies that Macdonald first suggested to Lewis, still then a resolute agnostic, that his quest for Joy and his sense of a lost childhood might both be pointing him toward Christianity.

When Lewis says that Macdonald baptized his imagination (*SBJ* 181), he is not referring to some sort of conversion experience. Lewis affirmed the medieval model of human personality, which can be envisioned as three concentric circles. At the center is the will, with intellect in the second circle, and imagination in the outer circle. (See *SL,* letter 6.) Though his imagination had been baptized by Macdonald, he would not consider himself a Christian until many years later, when his intellect had been satisfied and, lastly and most difficultly, when he had surrendered his will.

Lewis was also attracted by the writings of G. K. Chesterton, especially *Everlasting Man.* He enjoyed Chesterton not only for his robust humor but also for a sense of sincere goodness evident from his books. Finding an unexpected cogency in Chesterton's outline of history, Lewis began to feel that "Christianity itself was very sensible 'apart from its Christianity' " (*SBJ* 223). This paradox was deepened when Lewis began to realize that most of the authors he found intellectually nourishing (Spenser, Milton, Johnson, Macdonald, among others) took seriously "Christian mythology," while those who "did not suffer from religion" (Voltaire, Gibbon, Mill, Wells, Shaw) seemed thin and "tinny" by comparison (213–14). More and more it seemed that the profound writers were profoundly deluded by their faith, but the clear-seeing unbelievers did not see very far.

Moreover, several of the men at Oxford whom Lewis was most attracted to were also practicing Christians. First he met Neville Coghill, "clearly the most intelligent and best-informed man" among the undergraduates he met, who turned out to be a Christian and "a thoroughgoing supernaturalist" (*SBJ* 212). Later, when Lewis became a fellow at Magdalen College, Oxford, he got to know J. R. R. Tolkien and Hugo Dyson, two more kindred spirits who turned out to be Christians.

More and more, the two problems of Christian belief vs. unbelief and intellect vs. imagination became one problem. As late as 1927, ten years after he had arrived at Oxford, Lewis recorded in a diary his personal restiveness and philosophical turmoil, clearly linking the two dilemmas that continued to dominate his thoughts: "[Today I] was thinking about imagination and intellect and the unholy muddle I am in about them at present: undigested scraps of anthroposophy and psychoanalysis jostling with orthodox idealism over a background of good old Kirkian rationalism. Lord, what a mess! And all the time (with me) there's the danger of falling back into most childish superstitions, or of running into dogmatic materialism to escape them" (*DCSL* 431–32).

Lewis's resolution to these questions came over a period of about five years, culminating in his "reconversion" (the term he used) to Christianity in 1931. One of the important milestones in this process was a late night, almost all-night, talk with Tolkien and Dyson in September of that year. The two of them, who shared Lewis's reverence for myth, romance, and fairy tale, showed him that mythology revealed its own kind of truth and that Christianity was true mythology. Lewis had insisted that myths were nothing more than "lies breathed through silver," but Tolkien and Dyson answered that myth was better understood as "a real though unfocused gleam of divine truth falling on human imagination" (*Mir* 139). They argued that one of the great and universal myths, that of the Dying God who sacrifices himself for the people, showed an innate awareness of the need for redemption, not by one's own works, but as a gift from some higher realm. For them, the Incarnation was the pivotal point at which myth became history. The life, death, and resurrection of Christ not only fulfilled Old Testament types but also embodied—literally—central motifs found in all the world's mythologies. (Their arguments had been anticipated five years earlier, in 1926, when a fellow don of Lewis, whom he considered a hard-boiled atheist, commented that the evidence for the historicity of the Gospels was surprisingly good. "Rum thing," the skeptic had concluded. "All that stuff of Frazer's about the Dying God. Rum thing. It almost looks as if it had really happened once" [*SBJ* 223–24].)

No interpretive scheme could have been more liberating for Lewis. He had been trapped between an imagination that gloried in nature, myth, and romance and an intellect that dismissed it all as a tale told by an idiot, signifying nothing. This theory interpreted the functions of imagination and the intellect as complementary, not as competitive. Lewis would later call imagination "the organ of meaning" and intellect "the organ of truth."[13] The first generates pictures, metaphors, and myths by which we understand the world. The second weighs, sifts, and analyzes, discerning which products of the imagination correspond most closely with reality.

Apart from reconciling imagination and intellect, the paradigms offered by Tolkien and Dyson also helped Lewis justify his lifelong love of mythology and to validate his increasing attraction to Christianity. No more were his beloved Greek myths, Nordic sagas, and Irish legends mere escapist tripe unworthy of a thinking person. They became reservoirs of transrational truths; they provided insights, admittedly partial and distorted, about realities inaccessible to the unaided intellect. In Christianity, the True Myth to which all the others were pointing, Lewis would eventually find a worldview that he could defend as both good and real. It was a faith grounded in history and one with a reasonableness he never tired of defending. For Lewis it also became the fountainhead of all myths and tales of enchantment, the key to all mythologies, the myth that unfolded itself in history. About a month after Lewis's conversation with Tolkien and Dyson, he described a new book he had discovered by William Law, an eighteenth-century devotional writer, as "one of those rare works which make you say of Christianity, 'Here is the very thing you like in poetry and the romances, but this time it's true' " (*LCSL* 143).

When Lewis became a Christian, he also ended his quest to grasp Joy and resolved the "dialectic of desire" (*SBJ* 219) that he had been puzzling over since childhood. If, as Christian doctrine teaches, all humans are exiles from paradise, then how natural that they should feel pangs of longing, painful in their fallenness, yet pleasurable in that they point to genuine realities in which they may someday partake. In *Surprised by Joy,* Lewis says that once he became a believer again, his intense interest in *Sehnsucht* receded. He came to feel that it was not really Joy he had been seeking but rather "the naked Other, imageless (though our imagination salutes it with a hundred images), unknown, undefined, desire" (221). Having baptized his imagination with Christian myth years earlier, and then having satisfied his intellect, it only remained for Lewis to surrender his will. This was no small task, since he felt he was not simply accepting a body of doctrines but submitting to a living person: "Amiable agnostics will talk cheerfully about 'man's search for God.' To me, as I then was, they might as well have talked about the mouse's search for the cat. . . . Remember, I had always wanted, above all things, not to be 'interfered with.' I had wanted (mad wish) 'to call my soul my own.' . . . Total surrender, the absolute leap in the dark, were demanded" (227–28). Eventually, Lewis was able to do that which he felt was demanded of him. His eventual conversion to Christianity came in two stages. During the Trinity term of 1929 he knelt and prayed, yielding himself to a God whom he had not yet clearly defined, "the most dejected and reluctant convert in all England" (228–29). Then in 1931, three days after his talk with Tolkien and Dyson about myth, he accepted the doctrine of the Incarnation, affirming that Jesus of Nazareth was the Son of God (237). This represents the end of Lewis's account of his conversion, though it marks the beginning of his singular career as a critic, scholar, apologist, and imaginative writer.

After the publication of *Surprised by Joy,* Lewis reported with amusement that one of his friends wanted to write a supplement entitled "Suppressed by Jack" (*TST* 540). In shaping the story of his early life the way he did, Lewis left out a great deal of fascinating material that would have appeared in a more traditionally structured autobiography. Yet *Surprised by Joy* illuminates the master motifs of the Ransom stories, such as the reality of myth, the search for Joy, and the recovery of childhood. And as seen in terms such as *nurse, boy,* and *moonlight,* it also aids in interpreting recurring images in the trilogy by giving readers a more exact sense of their emotional associations for Lewis.

2

"Smuggled Theology": The Christian Vision of the Trilogy

All that is made seems planless to the darkened mind, because there are more plans than it looked for.

C. S. Lewis, *Perelandra*

THE DEDICATION of *Out of the Silent Planet* reads: "To my brother W. H. L./a life-long critic of the space-and-time story." This tribute to Warren Lewis seems straightforward enough, but it contains a double entendre that his brother and the other Inklings must have enjoyed. Jack sometimes used "space-and-time story" as a synonym for science fiction or fantasy.[1] But he also used "space-and-time" to refer to the physical universe, the only reality admitted by materialist philosophers. For Warren to be "a lifelong critic of the space-and-time story" meant he was a seasoned reader of the sort of book Jack had written; it also identified him as one who had long suspected that the physical universe is not "the whole show." This little inside joke is a synecdoche of the entire trilogy: Lewis offers his readers some lively specimens of interplanetary fantasy. But he also means to plant in their imaginations a suggestion that there may be more things in heaven and earth than are dreamt of in their philosophies.

As shown in the previous chapter, metaphysics for Lewis was not a natural starting point but rather the culmination of thirty years of experience. Critics usually assume that Lewis deliberately chose fantasy literature as an imaginative instrument to express his Christian vision. But the truth is just the reverse: Lewis did not simply adopt fantasy as a didactic vehicle after his conversion; rather it was his love of fantasy, myth, and romance that led him to Christianity in the first place. In the trilogy he recapitulates this process for his readers: first he tries to enchant them with fantasy worlds of wonder and danger, battlefields of good and evil; then gradually he reveals a correlation between these new, absorbing fantasies and some old doctrines whose familiarity may have bred contempt in his readers, or at least indifference. The recovery of childhood things that Lewis himself experienced is one he wants to pass on to others.

The actual writing of the trilogy began in 1937. Lewis and his good friend J. R. R. Tolkien agreed that there simply were not enough of their favorite sort of stories available, so they decided to try their own hand at it. Lewis proposed that each should write an "excursionary thriller," his a space-story and Tolkien's a time-story, both leading to the discovery of Myth.[2] Accordingly, Tolkien began a story called "The Lost Road," and Lewis, composing much more rapidly, completed a draft of *Out of the Silent Planet,* reading it in installments at weekly meetings of the Inklings. Lewis sent the manuscript first to J. M. Dent and Sons, who returned it. Then he sent it to Allen and Unwin, who had published Tolkien's *Hobbit.* Again it was not accepted, despite a letter from Tolkien defending it against some rather woolly minded criticisms from the publisher's reader. (This letter remains one of the most perceptive brief treatments of Lewis's strengths and weaknesses as a writer.)[3] The manuscript was then accepted by a house in London called the Bodley Head, who published it in the autumn of 1938.

Out of the Silent Planet was widely reviewed, but only a few commentators noticed the theological implications of the story. The year after the first book of the trilogy was published, Lewis wrote to a friend: "You will be both grieved and amused to hear that out of about 60 reviews only 2 showed any knowledge that my idea of the fall of the Bent One was anything but an invention of my own. But if there only was someone with a richer talent and more leisure I think that this great ignorance might be a help to the evangelisation of England; any amount of theology can now be smuggled into people's minds under cover of romance without their knowing it" (*LCSL* 167).

Such smuggling, of course, is exactly what Lewis did. Readers who may have missed the theological references in *Out of the Silent Planet* would find them even more explicit in *Perelandra* and *That Hideous Strength.*

Lewis's mention of only two reviews in sixty sounds hyperbolic, but a survey of *Out of the Silent Planet* reviews confirms his reckoning as essentially accurate. One reviewer, for example, confesses that he read *Out of the Silent Planet* twice and still could find no allegorical significance.[4] Another concludes that "*Out of the Silent Planet,* beautifully written as some of it is, does not seem quite to have grown from any conviction."[5]

One can hardly imagine a more inaccurate observation. *Out of the Silent Planet* is written with all of Lewis's convictions, with his whole worldview, in the background. He began the trilogy as a deliberate critique of what he called Evolutionism, a philosophy that projects Darwinism into the metaphysical sphere, speculating that humankind may eventually evolve into its own species of divinity, jumping from planet to planet and star to star. H. G. Wells was probably the most articulate and widely read proponent of this philosophy, so Lewis set out to create a Wellsian fantasy with a counter-Wellsian theme. Though one finds the idea of Evolutionism in Olaf Stapledon, G. B. Shaw, and C. H. Waddington, Lewis said that Evolutionism could, with some justice, be dubbed "Wellsianity" (*CR* 71).

Lewis began the Ransom trilogy because he feared that Evolutionism was beginning to capture the popular imagination. Soon after the publication of *Out of the Silent Planet,* he wrote to Roger Lancelyn Green, later to become his biographer: "What immediately spurred me to write was Olaf Stapledon's *Last and First Men* [1930], and an essay in J. B. S. Haldane's *Possible Worlds* [1927], both of which seemed to take the idea of such travel seriously and to have the desperately immoral outlook which I try to pillory in Weston. I like the whole inter-planetary idea as a *mythology* and simply wished to conquer for my own (Christian) point of view what has hitherto been used by the opposite side."[6] The following year Lewis explained to another correspondent who had asked about the origins of *Out of the Silent Planet:* "The danger of 'Westonism' I meant to be real. What set me about writing the book was the discovery that a pupil of mine took all that dream of interplanetary colonization quite seriously, and the realization that thousands of people in one way and another depend on some hope of perpetuating and improving the species for the whole meaning of the universe—that a 'scientific' hope of defeating death is a real rival to Christianity" (*LCSL* 166–67).

Last and First Men (1930), the first book mentioned above, offers Stapledon's prophetic panorama of our species' future, including an invasion of earth by cloud-creatures from Mars; the laboratory development of a new, improved type of humans, all brains and hands; the colonization of Venus and Neptune; and the eventual extinction of humanity two billion years in the future. Near the end of the story, one member of the species who represents almost pure intelligence explains the transcendent purpose that has guided all humans from continent to continent, and then planet to planet: "The task that was undertaken had to be completed. For the Scattering of the Seed has come for every one of us the supreme religious duty. Even those who continually sin against it recognize this as the last office of man."[7]

Last and First Men does not portray humans evolving into gods, even after two billion years. The closing pages offer a eulogy for Man, evoking, in haunting prose, the beauty of the species, but also its inescapable littleness.

> Great are the stars, and man is of no account to them. But man is a fair spirit, whom a star conceived and a star kills. He is greater than those bright blind companies. For though in them there is incalculable potentiality, in him there is achievement, small, but actual. Too soon, seemingly, he comes to his end. But when he is done he will not be nothing, not as though he had never been; for he is eternally a beauty in the eternal form of things.
>
> Man has winged hopefully. He had in him to go further than this

> short flight, now ending. He proposed even that he should become the Flower of All Things, and that he should learn to be the All-Knowing, the All-Admiring. Instead, he is to be destroyed. He is only a fledgling caught in a bush-fire. He is very small, very simple, very little capable of insight. His knowledge of the great orb of things is but a fledgling's knowledge. . . . The music of the spheres passes over him, through him, and is not heard. (303–4)

For someone like Lewis, this would represent the worst of all possible worlds. The philosophy of scattering the seed as a sacred obligation could easily justify experiments on animal and human subjects, as well as extermination of other species, whether on our own planet or on others. Yet even Stapledon seems to concede that such a goal serves no ultimate purpose. In the end he seems to agree with Bertrand Russell that "only on the firm foundation of unyielding despair can the soul's edifice henceforth be built."[8]

J. B. S. Haldane, the other writer whom Lewis hoped to answer in *Out of the Silent Planet,* was a Cambridge biochemist who championed the cause of science against those in the humanities and the churches, whom he considered reactionaries. Haldane was something of a latter-day Jeremy Bentham, an uncompromising logician who tended to tackle ethical and aesthetic questions in terms of utility and efficiency. In his little book *Callinicus* (1925), for example, he offers a vigorous, if chilling, defense of chemical warfare as no more inhumane than conventional weapons. In *Possible Worlds* (1927), he argues for scientific research on animals, noting that those opposed to his laboratory experiments on rats would probably not think twice about poisoning rats that had infested the family home. (Lewis, for one, was consistent in this regard: he was an antivivisectionist and also one who never set traps for the mice in his rooms at Oxford [*LTC* 32].)

The essay in *Possible Worlds* that unsettled Lewis was one entitled "Man's Destiny" (*LCSL* 160). There Haldane rhapsodizes about "man's taking his own evolution in hand" and of the possibilities of our species literally conquering the cosmos.

> In the improbable event of man taking his own evolution in hand—in other words, of improving human nature, as opposed to environ-

> ment—I can see no bounds at all to his progress. Less than a million years hence the average man or woman will realise all the possibilities that human life has so far shown. He or she will never know a minute's illness. He will be able to think like Newton, to write like Racine, to paint like Fra Angelico, to compose like Bach. He will be as incapable of hatred as St. Francis, and when death comes at the end of a life probably measured in thousands of years he will meet it with as little fear as Captain Oates or Arnold Von Winkelried. And every minute of his life will be lived with all the passion of a lover or a discoverer. We can form no idea whatever of the exceptional men of such a future.
>
> Men will certainly attempt to leave the earth. The first voyagers into interstellar space will die. . . . There is no reason why their successors should not succeed in colonising some, at least, of the other planets of our system, and ultimately the planets, if such exist, revolving around other stars than our sun. There is no theoretical limit to man's material progress but the subjection to complete conscious control of every atom and every quantum of radiation in the universe. There is, perhaps, no limit at all to his intellectual and spiritual progress. (304–5)

Such visions for the future, which now seem rather quixotic, appeared to Lewis as potentially very dangerous. The idea that humans may one day evolve into *Übermensch* was for Lewis the latest variant of the serpent's temptation to Eve: "Ye shall be as gods" (Gen. 3:5, KJV). A program of helping evolution do its work could also be used to justify all manner of atrocities against other species or against "inferior" members of the human species. Such a theory comes dangerously close to Hitler's dream of a "master race," a parallel that Lewis underscores in *That Hideous Strength.*

Apart from debunking Evolutionism, Lewis also hoped that taking his readers on an imaginative voyage to another world would give them a new perspective on this one. Charles Moorman has stated the underlying strategy of the trilogy most succinctly: "Lewis's main aim in the creation of the silent-planet myth is to create and maintain a metaphor that will serve to carry in fictional form the basic tenets of Christianity and present them from a non-Christian point of view, but without reference to normal Christian symbols."[9] Though his initial impulse for writing interplanetary romance may not have been quite as calculatedly didactic as Moorman suggests, Lewis does portray a cosmos ruled by a Triune god, whose loyal subjects—angels and human—must daily battle the dark and fallen rulers of this world. In fact, Lewis's fictional representations are re-presentations of the central doctrines of Christian myth.

Out of the Silent Planet

In the first book of the trilogy, the theological dimension of the story is not revealed until nearly halfway through the novel. Once Ransom escapes Weston and Devine, who had abducted him and carried him off to Malacandra (Mars), he befriends the otterlike creatures of Malacandra called hrossa and learns some of their speech. A pious man, he begins to wonder if he should undertake to instruct them in his faith. But they have their own definite convictions, and it is they who marvel at his ignorance. They tell him that they are ruled by Oyarsa, who is himself subject to Maleldil the Younger, who created their world and who lives with the Old One. Ransom also learns that three of the species on the planet are called hnau (67–68).

After further conversations with a second of the rational species, the sorns (102), and with the Oyarsa of Malacandra (120–21), Ransom comes to understand that Maleldil the Younger created the Field of Arbol (solar system) and all the beings in it. He chose an Oyarsa, or tutelary intelligence, to rule each world, served by nearly imperceptible beings called eldila. However, on the third planet, the Oyarsa and some of his eldils rose up in rebellion against Maleldil, recognizing no authority but themselves. Led by the Bent Oyarsa, this world was now cut off from the others and thus called Thulcandra, "the Silent Planet." It remains a battleground, though there are rumors in Deep Heaven of wondrous things performed by Maleldil to reclaim his lost world.

This is certainly the stuff of science fiction. It is also orthodox Christian theology, though with a distinctly medieval hue. In response to inquiries about the trilogy's symbolism, Lewis explained straightforwardly that Maleldil the Elder and Younger represented the Father and the Son of Christian theology, that eldils represented angels, and the Bent One was Satan.[10] Lest it seem blasphemous to add new chapters to Christian doctrine, he also explained that his stories were a form of "imagining out loud," speculations in fiction about "what God might be supposed to have done in other worlds" (*LCSL* 261).

Lewis's strategy here is an ambitious one, and critics differ about how successfully he is able to blend fantasy and theology. But part of what makes his approach intriguing is the way the theological implications of Ransom's adventures emerge by "progressive revelation." As attested by the reviewers quoted above, a good many readers can finish *Out of the Silent Planet* without ever identifying Maleldil with God. Or for that matter they may finish the book without recognizing the thematic implications of the Oyarsa, the eldils, or the creatures called hnau.

For one thing, readers may be confused by the name "Maleldil." If eldils are angels, then "Maleldil" suggests the meaning "bad angel." Obviously, this title does not fit a benevolent divinity, so critics have expended a great deal of ingenuity trying to unlock the meaning of the name. William Norwood suggests that it might stand for "male eldil," since maleness in hierarchical societies is associated with higher authority.[11] J. R. Christopher finds its roots in Anglo-Saxon *mal,* "an agreement or judgment" and *ealdor,* "lord," interpreting the name to mean "Lord of Judgment" or "Lord of the Agreement/Covenant."[12] Perhaps most convincing is Evan Gibson's speculation that "Mal" is taken from the Hebrew word for "king," so that "Maleldil" means "king of all spirits," or more familiarly, "Lord of Hosts."[13] Lewis himself said that he knew of no conscious connections between the language of Malacandra and actual languages, saying he wanted the words to have "emotional, not intellectual suggestiveness." He added that the quality in the name "Maleldil" that appealed to him was its liquidity (*LCSL* 284). Perhaps it is best to let the matter rest there.

Readers who do sense parallels between Maleldil and the God of Christianity may still be puzzled by the Oyarsa and his eldils. Neither of these seems to fit the usual notions of angels. Lewis explains at the end of the story that the word *Oyarses* comes from Bernardus Silvestris, a twelfth-century Platonist. The Oyarsa is the tutelary spirit of the planet, a higher order of angel responsible to rule that sphere (152).

Some early readers of *Out of the Silent Planet* thought the Oyarsa was Lewis's image of God,[14] but that is a careless reading. The hrossa tell Ransom that Maleldil made and ruled their world and that the Oyarsa is subject to him (68). Far from being omniscient, the Oyarsa of Malacandra wants to hear from Ransom what Maleldil has done on earth, the silent planet. He wants Ransom to confirm stories that Maleldil "has taken strange counsel and dared terrible things, wrestling with the Bent One in Thulcandra" (121). And when Ransom explains the traditions he knows on the subject, the Oyarsa shows that even a majestic spirit like himself can be awed by the deeds of Maleldil: "You have shown me more wonders than are known in the whole of heaven" (142).

The wonders Ransom told the Oyarsa about were the life, death, and resurrection of Christ, which atoned for the sin of Adam and broke the power of the Bent One. To confirm that this is what Lewis has in mind, note the Oyarsa's phrasing about his wanting to hear what Maleldil has done on Thulcandra: "It is a thing we desire to look into." This is taken word for word from 1 Peter 1:12, where the suffering of Christ and the glory that followed are described as "things which angels desire to look into." Here Lewis cleverly takes theological doctrines that readers might find dull or unpalatable and reshapes them into an interplanetary battle scenario more compelling than most of the science fiction available in the pulps.

The passage from 1 Peter also confirms that the Oyarsa and his eldils are Lewis's representations of angels, although we find no harps or halos on Malacandra. In fact, they are so unlike biblical or traditional pictures of angels that one young reader asked Lewis if they were supposed to represent fairies (*LTC* 70).

Lewis's portrayal of the eldila clearly illustrates his strategy of inviting readers to look at old doctrines with new eyes. He well knew that angels in the Bible are never portrayed with harps and halos. He reminded one reader that angels who appear in Scripture nearly always excite terror in those who see them and that the word *kherub* in Hebrew referred not to "horrid little fat baby 'cherubs' " but to a creature like the fabled Gryphon, with the body of a lion and wings of eagles (*LAL* 12–13).

In *The Discarded Image* Lewis laments the increasingly disappointing portrayal of angels he finds in Western literature. After the "unrivalled majesty" of Dante's angels come the classicist angels of Milton, with "too much anatomy and too much armour" and behaving too much like characters out of Homer or Virgil. After Milton, Lewis finds "total degradation," ending in "the purely consolatory, and hence waterishly feminine, angels of nineteenth century art" (75). In trying to find a model for his eldils, Lewis must have considered first what he considered to be the best portrayal of an angel in imaginative literature (*SMRL* 69): the heavenly messenger in the *Inferno* who strides through the fifth circle of hell on God's errand, parting the lost souls at his feet and opening the gate of Dis with just a wave of his hand (9, 76–103).

Lewis's eldils have some of the majesty and self-possession of Dante's stern messenger but none of his overwhelming presence. In fact, the eldils on Malacandra are just on the margins of perception. The first time Ransom comes near an eldil, he does not even see it (*OSP* 71). The next one he meets can hardly be distinguished from "imagination and the dance of sunlight on the lake" (79). Ransom's hrossan host explains: "*Eldila* are hard to see. They are not like us. Light goes through them. You must be looking in the right place and the right time; and that is not likely to come about unless the *eldil* wishes to be seen. Sometimes you can mistake them for a sunbeam or even a moving of the leaves; but when you look again you see that it was an *eldil* and that it is gone" (76). The closest that Ransom ever comes to seeing the eldils is when he journeys to the island city of Meldilorn to appear before the Oyarsa.

> The surface of the island was subject to tiny variations of light and shade which no change in the sky accounted for. . . . Like the silvery noises in the air, these footsteps of light were shy of observation. Where he looked hardest they were least to be seen: on the edges of his field of vision they came crowding as though a complex arrange-

> ment of them were there in progress. To attend to any one of them was to make it invisible, and the minute brightness seemed often to have just left the spot where his eyes fell. He had no doubt that he was "seeing"—as much as he would ever see—the *eldila.* (109)

If Lewis objected to the "waterishly feminine angels" of popular art, one wonders at first how it is an improvement to portray angels as hardly visible at all. People in the Bible indeed sometimes entertained angels unawares, but that is because the angels appeared as ordinary humans, not as "footsteps of light." So Lewis is attempting something here other than just trying to get back to biblical pictures of angels.

Our best clue to Lewis's narrative strategy here comes from a letter he wrote to two children who had asked about his eldils. Where most authors might offer a short reply, or none, Lewis gives his young admirers a concise lesson in angelology: "The view that angels have no bodies of any kind has not always been held among Christians. The old idea (early Middle Ages) was that they had bodies of aether as we have bodies of gross matter. The opposite view (your one) was that of the great scholastics—Albertus Magnus, Thomas Aquinas, etc. . . . Of course, I just took, for the purposes of a story, the one that seemed most imaginable. I have no scruples about this because, religiously, the question seems to me of no importance. And anyway what do we mean by 'matter'?" (*LTC* 73). This letter indicates that Lewis's eldils might be hard to see because they have bodies of ether, the lighter-than-air substance that, according to the medieval model, filled the spaces between the heavenly spheres.

But there is a larger purpose suggested by the examples of sunlight dancing on the lake or moving leaves or beams of brightness one can sense but not see. Lewis is hoping to "smuggle theology" into readers' minds, to baptize their imaginations. If his eldils appeared to Ransom clad in radiant garments and announced, "Fear not," their identity would be so recognizable as to be dismissible. But Lewis wants to subvert the reader's certainty about the barriers between the natural and the supernatural, between myth and history. He is hoping that, after finishing the trilogy, readers may give every peculiar slant of light a second look and think perhaps, "Why that's only the moonlight filtering through the trees—and yet for a moment . . ."

Besides reimaging what angels might be like, Lewis in *Out of the Silent Planet* reexamines what it means to be human. In his Malacandrian term *hnau,* he resurrects the Aristotelian concept of personhood. The hrossa explain to Ransom early on that he is *hnau,* that they are *hnau,* and the sorns and pfifltriggi are *hnau* (68). Since these are the species on the planet who use language, we initially assume that to be hnau is simply to be a rational being. But later when Weston shoots Hyoi, Ransom explains to his dying hrossan friend that humans are "only half *hnau*" (81). In the end, after the Oyarsa has heard Weston's grandiose but vapid speech about scattering the human seed throughout the cosmos, Oyarsa pronounces Weston to be a bent hnau, perhaps curable because he is at least motivated by some moral imperative, albeit a warped one. But the Oyarsa calls Devine "only a talking animal," motivated purely by greed, one in whom the hnau is already dead.

What Lewis means by hnau is stated most clearly not in *Out of the Silent Planet* but in *Perelandra.* There Ransom muses on "*animal rationale*—an animal, yet also a reasonable soul," which he calls "the old definition of Man" (207). To be hnau is to have a "reasonable soul," to have a rational sense and a moral sense. To be hnau is also to be made in the image of Maleldil (*OSP* 120). Ransom calls the bent race of humans on earth "half *hnau*" because their moral sense has become deformed, either by visionary schemes, like Weston's, or by cynical self-interest, like Devine's.

Lewis speculated that his word *hnau* may have been unconsciously influenced by the Greek word *nous,* "mind" (*LCSL* 284). His essay "Religion and Rocketry" further elaborates on the concept and also serves as a gloss on some of the major themes of *Out of the Silent Planet.* Written to address the theological implications of discovering life on other planets, "Religion and Rocketry" poses a series of questions: Are there living species on any planet except Earth? If so, do these species have "rational souls"? Lewis defines a rational soul as "not merely the faculty to abstract and calculate, but the apprehension of values, the power to mean by 'good' something more than 'good for me' or 'good for my species' " (*WLN* 85). (His wording here is particularly germane to *Out of the Silent Planet*, since for Devine "good" does mean "good for me," and for Weston "good" means "good for my species.") Assuming an affirmative answer to his first two questions, Lewis then speculates that other species besides humans may not have fallen. "Perhaps of all races *we* only fell. Perhaps Man is the only lost sheep" (87). He adds that the vast astronomical distances may be God's quarantine "to prevent the spiritual infection of a fallen species from spreading" (91).

Here, as so often in Lewis, he asks questions in his expository prose that he answers imaginatively in his fiction. In the Ransom trilogy he does indeed create species on other planets, rational and unfallen species. Only earth, the silent planet, is "infected" by evil—and the space flights of Weston threaten to spread the infection, as he brings untimely deaths to Malacandra and imperils the Eden of Perelandra.

Perelandra

Lewis commented that he wrote *Perelandra* for his "co-religionists" (*OOW* 78)—that is, fellow Christians. The theology in the second book of the trilogy is thus not smuggled in but carried in through the front door. *Perelandra* is the story of "Paradise Retained,"[15] of an Eve who is able to resist the tempter long enough for Ransom to destroy him. In fulfilling his quest, Ransom too learns a great deal about the reality of myth and how ordinary mortals may be called upon to engage in mythic labors.

Perelandra begins in much the same spirit in which *Out of the Silent Planet* ends. Again we meet Lewis himself as a character in the novel, this time trudging toward Ransom's cottage and worrying about getting involved in "inter-planetary politics" (10). "Lewis" muses that Ransom's discovery of creatures called eldils broke down one's comfortable distinction between natural and supernatural, exposing it as an arbitrary division used to ease "the burden of intolerable strangeness which this universe imposes on us" (11).

Lewis here sounds a keynote for the trilogy, his sense of unseen transcendent forces just beneath the surface of the workaday world.

Lewis uses a number of techniques to break down the distinction between his fictional world and our "factual" world. Most obviously, he uses his own name and those of other real people ("C.J." in *Out of the Silent Planet* and "Humphrey" in *Perelandra,* based upon his friend and personal physician, R. E. "Humphrey" Havard). He also quotes ancient authorities, such as the Bible and a medieval scholar Natvilcius, who assume the reality of eldils. He even appeals to human psychology early in *Perelandra:* "Lewis" learns that extreme anxiety he experienced in approaching Ransom's cottage was not just a case of the jitters or fear of the unknown; his mind was actually being beseiged by bent eldils who wanted him to turn back. Thus the author blurs the distinction between the "psychological" and the "spiritual."

Lewis's stress on the connectedness of his fictional world and our own world contrasts sharply with the theory and practice of his good friend J. R. R. Tolkien. Tolkien believed that the highest calling of the fiction writer—especially the fantasy writer—was subcreation, the imaginative creation of secondary worlds independent of the primary world in which the author lived. As a devout Roman Catholic, Tolkien viewed subcreation as a form of worship, a way for creatures to express the divine image in them by becoming creators. Tolkien always stressed the independence of his created worlds; in over 1,500 pages of *The Lord of the Rings,* Tolkien studiously avoids any literary or historical allusions that would draw readers away from his fictive world and make them think of their own. Lewis subscribed in theory to Tolkien's doctrine of subcreation,[16] but in practice his fantasies always underscore the interpenetration of his secondary worlds and our primary world. Throughout the Ransom trilogy (as well as the Narnia chronicles), Lewis's strategy is to make readers sense that his fantasy world is more real than they might have supposed—and that their "real world" is more filled with the fantastic than they might have supposed.

The first theological link between Lewis's created world and the real world comes in *Perelandra* when Ransom first tells "Lewis" that he has been commissioned to travel to another planet to engage in some sort of combat with dark forces. To reassure "Lewis" that he has not succumbed to megalomania, Ransom refers to a Bible verse about fighting "principalities and powers" (23). The verse Ransom has in mind is Ephesians 6:12: "For we wrestle not against flesh and blood, but against principalities, against powers, against the rulers of the darkness of this world, against spiritual wickedness in high places" (KJV). Ransom correctly notes that the last phrase does not refer to highly placed human rulers, but rather to "hypersomatic beings at great heights" (24). "Hypersomatic" here means "beyond bodily form," and "great heights" means "in the heavenly world, in the supernatural sphere." So the dark eldils that Ransom and "Lewis" have to contend with are the same demonic powers with whom the apostle Paul predicted all Christians would have to wrestle.

Apart from experiencing the reality of biblical demons, Ransom discovers on Perelandra a great deal of truth in other mythologies as well. In his time on Malacandra, Ransom had already discovered that the classical deities Mars and Venus were pictures of the Oyarses of those planets (*OSP* 111). He began to suspect that "the distinction between history and mythology might be itself meaningless outside the Earth" (144–45). Once he arrives on Perelandra he discovers the truth of his suspicions and learns the theological significance of myth.

Awakening to his first morning on the planet, Ransom realizes that he has come upon the place pictured in myths of Paradise: "At Ransom's waking something happened to him which perhaps never happens to a man until he is out of his own world: he saw reality, and thought it was a dream. He opened his eyes and saw a strange heraldically coloured tree loaded with yellow fruits and silver leaves. Round the base of the indigo stem was coiled a small dragon covered with scales of red gold. He recognized the garden of the Hesperides at once" (45). The Garden of the Hesperides is the Greek equivalent to the Garden of Eden. Recalling his earlier experiences on Malacandra, Ransom asks himself again, "Were all the things which appeared as mythology on earth scattered through other worlds as realities?" (45). Even before encountering the Green Lady, this planet's Eve, he already has a sense that he was not following an adventure but enacting a myth (47).

When Ransom does meet the Green Lady, she is—like her world—the embodiment of many mythologies.

> Opposites met in her and were fused in a fashion for which we have no images. One way of putting it would be to say that neither our sacred nor our profane art could make her portrait. Beautiful, naked, shameless, young—she was obviously a goddess: but then the face . . . like the sudden coldness and stillness of a church when we enter it from a hot street—that made her a Madonna. The alert, inner silence which looked out from those eyes overawed him; yet at any moment she might laugh like a child, or run like Artemis or dance like a Maenad. (64)

Gradually, after recognizing that he has been sent to Perelandra to prevent the mythic fall of this new Eve, Ransom comes to understand the connection between our world's myths and otherworldly realities: "Long since on Mars, and more strongly since he came to Perelandra, Ransom had been perceiving that the triple distinction of truth from myth and of both from fact was purely terrestrial—was part and parcel of that unhappy division between soul and body which resulted from the Fall. Even on earth the sacraments existed as a permanent reminder that the division was neither wholesome nor final. The Incarnation had been the beginning of its disappearance. In Perelandra it would have no meaning at all" (143–44). Here we find Lewis reiterating the paradigms that were so influential in his own conversion: the truth embodied in myths, and Christianity as the greatest and truest of all myths. Lewis called *Perelandra* his favorite of all the books he had written (*LTC* 95), and that may well be because he found in this book his most satisfying blend of intellect and imagination. If all mythologies suggested the need for a Dying God to redeem a lost people, the Incarnation literally fulfilled that need. If all mythologies revealed the human longing for some lost paradise, Ransom had literally found it on Perelandra.

But Ransom is called to do more than experience myth on

Perelandra; he must enact it—to do battle with the Un-man and try to destroy him. This development in the story has disturbed a good many readers. After all, the entire middle section of *Perelandra* is framed as a "novel of ideas." In this genre, the protagonist is supposed to defeat his or her opponents by strength of mind, not strength of arms. The Right Thinkers are supposed to demolish their enemies by superior arguments, not by crushing their skulls. Is Lewis implying that Christians abandon the battle of ideas and go knock a few infidels over the head?

Lewis tries to anticipate this objection by having it occur first to Ransom himself. As he contemplates physical combat, Ransom's responds that "no such crude, materialistic struggle could possibly be what Maleldil really intended. . . . It would degrade the spiritual warfare to the condition of mere mythology" (143). He then comes to see that he himself is taking part in myth, that the distinction between myth and history occurs only on the fallen planet. He may only be Elwin Ransom of Cambridge on earth, but on Perelandra he will be remembered as a kind of Beowulf who slew Grendel. (And we do not consider it unseemly that Beowulf slew Grendel rather than trying to rehabilitate him.)

Lewis's strategy of having ordinary people enter into the mythic realm works more successfully in the Narnia chronicles than it does in *Perelandra.* It is delightful to see how the Pevensie children, so unexceptionable on earth, become legendary kings and queens in Narnia. But in *Perelandra,* the transition from "novel of ideas," where battles are won with words, to mythic fantasy, where one seeks to destroy one's enemies physically, is not made smoothly or convincingly enough.

One Lewis critic, Ed Chapman, asserts that Ransom should have performed an exorcism on Weston instead of killing him.[17] But another critic, Evan K. Gibson, reminds us that Ransom is not attempting to destroy Weston the scientist. He seeks to destroy the Un-Man, a ghost in a machine, a demon—perhaps the devil himself—using a human body in an unholy incarnation.[18] The Weston whose philosophy Ransom detests need no longer be refuted. That Weston disappeared after the apparently fatal seizure that followed his grandiose proclamation, "I *am* the Universe. I, Weston, am your God and your Devil. I call that Force into me completely" (96). "That Force" did indeed enter in completely, and it is this dark force that now makes use of Weston's body. As Ransom notes, the Weston after the convulsion did not look like a sick man, but rather a dead one. "Weston's body was kept, walking and undecaying, in Perelandra by some wholly different kind of life, and . . . Weston himself was gone" (110).

As will be shown in chapter 6, the Un-man also represents a side of Ransom himself that must be expunged. The destruction of the Un-man resolves the major external conflict of the story, but it also betokens the end of the conflict that has been raging within Ransom's own mind and heart.

When the protracted combat is finally over, Ransom has been wounded in the heel, but he has crushed the Un-man's head. These wounds allude to Genesis 3:15, where God curses the serpent just after the Fall.

> And I will put enmity
>   between you and the woman,
>   and between your offspring and hers;
> he will crush your head,
>   and you will strike his heel. (NIV)

In the immediate context in Genesis, the events in Eden are evoked to explain the fact that humans and snakes have never coexisted very peacefully. But Christian theologians have long interpreted this verse as the first great adumbration of *Heilsgeschichte,* "sacred history," a promise that a Redeemer would come to atone for Adam and Eve's sin by crushing Satan's head after being wounded by him.

Indeed Ransom's adventure on Perelandra has a number of parallels with the mission of Christ on earth: he enters naked into a world in order to fulfill God's purpose for it; he has a dual nature like Christ (who is totally God and totally man, according to Christian creeds); he is tempted to give up his mission; he undergoes a kind of Gethsemane of anxiety and loneliness the night before he must suffer; he undergoes a symbolic death and rebirth in being dragged down below the surface and spending three days there; he reemerges to have his mission celebrated by others; and then he returns to his former sphere.

All of these parallels have confused some readers. For if Ransom is the symbolic Christ of Perelandra, then what of Maleldil the Younger? Those who may not have recognized Maleldil as a figure of Christ in *Out of the Silent Planet* are given even more explicit clues in *Perelandra.* Ransom muses on the mythic significance of Maleldil being born a man at Bethlehem (144) and makes a grave marker for Weston that says Weston was born 1,896 revolutions around the sun since the son Maleldil was born as a hnau in Thulcandra (188).

One of Lewis's readers wrote him about the seeming redundancy of Christ figures in *Perelandra,* and he answered in his usual obliging, nonevasive way: "Ransom (to some extent) plays the role of Christ not because he allegorically represents Him (as Cupid represents falling in love) but because in reality every real Christian is really called upon in some measure to *enact* Christ. Of course Ransom does this rather more spectacularly than most. But that does not mean that he does it allegorically. It only means that fiction (at any rate my kind of fiction) chooses extreme cases" (*LCSL* 283). This theme is most clearly suggested on the night of Ransom's personal Gethsemane, when the Voice tells him, "It is not for nothing that you are named Ransom" (147). As Ransom muses on the etymology of his name, the Voice adds, "My name is also Ransom" (148). (Readers who wonder if Lewis had this meaning in mind all along should know that Ransom's name in the version Lewis originally submitted for publication was "Unwin." When he first submitted the manuscript to Unwin and Allen, he changed the name to Ransom.)[19]

That Hideous Strength

In the third book of the trilogy, Lewis completes the theological unveiling that began in *Perelandra.* Before the narrative even begins, he acknowledges the theological dimension of his story: instead of talking about good eldils and bent ones in the preface, he states on the first page that *That Hideous Strength* concerns angels and devils and that the book was written in response to some disturbing notions he had encountered in talking to a scientific colleague and later in the works of Olaf Stapledon (7).

As shown earlier, Stapledon's *Last and First Men,* with its doctrine of humanity's sacred obligation to scatter its seed among other worlds, provided the impetus for Lewis to start writing the trilogy in the first place. In *That Hideous Strength* Lewis goes beyond *Out of the Silent Planet* in trying to expose the fallacies and dangers in the philosophy of "Westonism." By the time he composed the third book of the trilogy, Lewis had read Stapledon's other well-known novel, *Star Maker* (1937), which surveys the entire history of the cosmos and suggests that some sort of god, or creative principle, is evolving amid the galaxies. Writing to Arthur C. Clarke in 1943, Lewis described the ending of Stapledon's novel as "sheer devil worship."[20]

The protagonists of *That Hideous Strength* are Mark and Jane Studdock, a pair of anchorless modern intellectuals in an unfulfilling marriage, who undergo diametrically opposite pilgrimages as the story unfolds. As Mark works his way through the "wheels within wheels" at the National Institute of Coordinated Experiments (N.I.C.E.), readers find there too a progression from scientific pragmatism, to Evolutionism, to "sheer devil worship." At the lowest level are functionaries like Busby and Curry, who think the purpose of N.I.C.E. is to provide centralized organization for scientific research. Busby calls N.I.C.E. "the first attempt to take applied science seriously from the national point of view" (37), while Curry burbles about putting "science itself on a scientific basis" (38). Lord Feverstone (Devine) laughs at these simpleminded marionettes and explains the goals of N.I.C.E. to Mark in Weston-esque terms: to continue interplanetary expansion; to rid the planet of species that compete with humans for resources; and to purify the human species itself, through "sterilization of the unfit [and] liquidation of backward races" (42). (The parallels between the animating ideas of N.I.C.E. and those of Nazism would certainly not be lost on the novel's original readers in 1945.)

Even more radical than Feverstone are those at N.I.C.E., like Filostrato, who want to dispense with organic life altogether, retaining only Mind (173), and Straik, who offers Mark "the unspeakable glory of being present at the creation of God Almighty" (179). Readers who think that Lewis is resorting to caricature tactics here will find similar ideas in Haldane, Stapledon, and Shaw and in more recent writers like Ray Bradbury and Arthur C. Clarke.

To explain the intellectual climate in which such diverse, and sometimes outré, notions could come together, the narrator probes the thoughts of Ransom, who leads the opposition against N.I.C.E.: "The physical sciences, good and innocent in themselves, had . . . begun to be warped, had been subtly manoeuvred in a certain direction. Despair of objective truth had been increasingly insinuated into the scientists; indifference to it, and a concentration upon mere power, had been the result. . . . Dreams of the far future destiny of man were dragging up from its shallow and unquiet grave the old dream of Man as God" (203). The narrator continues, perhaps with an excess of exposition, explaining why positivists in the tradition of Huxley (and Kirkpatrick) should not be shocked by where their ideas are leading: "What should they find incredible, since they no longer believed in a rational universe? What should they regard as too obscene, since they held that all morality was a mere subjective by-product of the physical and economic situations of men?" (203).

Looking back after nearly a half century, it seems ironic that Lewis's apprehensions would be more fully realized in his own discipline, in the study of literary texts, than in the sciences. The work of Thomas Kuhn and others concerning the subjectivity of the scientific paradigms seems to have been more warmly received by scholars in the humanities than by scientists themselves. Perhaps the trait that most unites poststructuralist approaches to literature is a "despair of objective truth" and a "concentration upon mere power."

The ideas touched upon in *That Hideous Strength* are more fully developed in Lewis's book-length essay *The Abolition of Man.* There he makes the case for objective moral values and objective aesthetic values. Lewis begins by taking to task the writers of an elementary textbook who teach that when one calls a waterfall sublime, one is actually saying, "This waterfall induces sublime feelings in me." Sublimity, according to them, is a label for an emotional state; it is not anything in nature but something imputed by human minds upon the environment. Lewis argues that such an approach reduces all value judgments to mere expressions of emotion, largely irrelevant in serious discussion (15).

Against this climate of relativism and imputed value, Lewis harkens back to the traditional model: "Until quite modern times all teachers and even all men believed the universe to be such that certain emotional reactions on our part could be either congruous or incongruous to it—believed, in fact, that objects did not merely receive, but could *merit,* our approval or disapproval, our reverence, or our contempt" (*AM* 25). Lewis quotes Plato, Aristotle, Confucius, Augustine, and others to show that traditionally moral education has been defined as a process of learning to conform one's sentiments to the acknowledged pattern of the universe. Though this pattern is assumed by all religious traditions, according to Lewis, he borrows the concept of the Way from Taoism: "The Chinese also speak of a great thing (the greatest thing) called the *Tao.* It is the reality beyond all predicates, the abyss that was before the Creator Himself. It is Nature, it is the Way, the Road. It is the Way in which the universe goes on, the Way in which things everlastingly emerge, stilly and tranquilly, into space and time. It is also the Way which every man should tread in imitation of that cosmic and supercosmic progression, conforming all activities to that great exemplar" (28).

Such analysis is unabashedly essentialist. Depending upon one's own response to the contemporary climate of poststructuralist analysis, *The Abolition of Man* may seem woefully naive and obsolete, or else it may seem a prescient forewarning of trends that would become much more radical after Lewis's time. If Lewis could hear current discussions that assume that not only values but also meanings are radically indeterminate, he might sigh, "Après moi, le déluge."

Regardless of how cogent one finds Lewis's central thesis, his choice of the sublimity of waterfalls may not be the best example from which to argue his case. History does provide examples of changes in the general sensibility, changes that are evident in the artistic artifacts produced by a culture. Before Romanticism in Western Europe, we do not find poems celebrating the stern magnificence of mountains or paintings of "empty" landscapes. If eighteenth-century travelers had had cameras, they would probably not have taken pictures of many of the things that modern tourists take for granted as "beautiful."

In *The Abolition of Man* Lewis generally makes a stronger case for axiomatic moral values than for unchanging aesthetic values. He also notes, however, that one cannot arrive at value judgments using reason alone. In between the head (reason) and the belly (the appetites) must come the chest—the seat of magnanimity, of "Sentiment," of "emotions organized by trained habits into stable sentiments" (34). Lewis calls these "the indispensable liaison officers between cerebral man and visceral man." In fact, he says, these may be the defining trait of humans, for by intellect they are mere spirit and by appetites they are mere animal (34). Those who deny the reality of sentiment, of objective values, are—in Lewis's term—"men without chests."

In *That Hideous Strength* virtually all of the technocrats at N.I.C.E. would qualify as people "without chests." In their disregard for traditional moral norms, for natural beauty, for the suffering of animals and of other humans, they reduce all questions of value to matters of rationality, utility, or self-interest. They dismiss any ethical qualms about what they are doing with grandiose abstractions about the advancement of the species (258), or else they dismiss such qualms as meaningless biochemical events (296).

In order to make inroads at N.I.C.E., Mark Studdock must continually suppress his natural instincts and his better judgment.

He moves from the merely vulgar to the unethical and then to the criminal, but he stops short of sacrificing his wife to the ambitions of his superiors. Placed in the "Objective Room," a chamber whose proportions and furnishings are designed to subvert his sense of normality, Mark's instincts carry him in the opposite direction: "That idea of the Straight or the Normal which had occurred to him during his first visit to this room, grew stronger and more solid in his mind till it had become a kind of mountain. He had never before known what an Idea meant: he had always thought till now that they were things inside one's own head. But now, when his head was continually attacked and often completely filled with the clinging corruption of the training, this Idea towered up above him—something which obviously existed quite independently of himself" (310). Though the narrator declares that Mark's modern education had provided him with "hardly one rag of noble thought, either Christian or Pagan" (185), he still has an inborn sense of some reality towering above all the reductionistic rhetoric at N.I.C.E.

Later, when he is commanded by Frost to trample a crucifix, Mark recognizes that he is in mortal danger, but some instinct deeper than self-preservation arises within him: "Christianity was a fable. It would be ridiculous to die for a religion one did not believe. This Man himself, on that very cross, had discovered it to be a fable, and had died complaining that the God in whom he trusted had forsaken him—had, in fact, found the universe a cheat. . . . If the universe was a cheat, was that a good reason for joining its side? Supposing the Straight was utterly powerless, always and everywhere certain to be mocked, tortured, and finally killed by the Crooked, what then? Why not go down with the ship?" (337). Mark refuses to trample on the cross, the first courageous thing he has ever done in his life. This is the beginning of his recovery. Stripped of all other supports and defenses, Mark's regeneration begins when he discovers that he has nothing left but the Way.

Like her husband, Jane Studdock will also be "shaken out of the modest little outfit of contemporary ideas which had hitherto made her portion of wisdom" (150). Mark discovers the Straight by the *via negativa,* by almost losing himself to the Crooked, the Perverse, the

Bent. Jane moves in the opposite direction as she is drawn closer to the community at St. Anne's.

Several critics have noted the structural symmetries in *That Hideous Strength* by which the Studdocks' opposite pilgrimages are marked. Jane begins with a malaise and lack of commitment, either to her marriage or to her scholarship; Mark begins with a reckless commitment, a headlong plunge to fulfill his ambitions by the shortest route possible. Jane dreams realities and thinks they are illusions; Mark is deluded about the actual workings of Bracton and N.I.C.E., just when he thinks he knows what is really going on. Jane takes a slow train to St. Anne's, while Mark rushes to Belbury in a big, flashy car driven by the reckless Feverstone. Jane is invited to join St. Anne's, while Mark is coerced into joining N.I.C.E. The fresh garden at St. Anne's fills Jane with images of paradise, while the garden at N.I.C.E. is artificial and sterile, like "a municipal cemetery" (101). Jane is filled with ineffable joy when she first meets the head of St. Anne's—the regal and mystical Ransom, returned from Perelandra. Mark is filled with unspeakable horror and revulsion when he meets the "head" of N.I.C.E.—a decapitated head supposedly kept alive by scientific apparatus but actually animated by dark eldils.[21]

Like Ransom in *Out of the Silent Planet,* revelations come to Jane bit by bit. First she learns that she is not a neurotic but a clairvoyant, one with the power to dream realities (64–65). Then she learns, begrudgingly, that she has contributed to her failing marriage as much as her husband (147). Then she discovers that Arthurian legends are truer than she ever could have imagined (176). Eventually, she undergoes a complete paradigm shift. On Malacandra Ransom had gradually come to realize that Maleldil was the same person as the God he already believed in. In *That Hideous Strength* Jane makes the even more startling discovery that Maleldil is the God she had not believed in.

> If it had ever occurred to her to question whether all these things might be the reality behind what she had been taught at school as "religion," she had put the thought aside. The distance between these alarming and operative realities and the memory, say, of fat

> Mrs. Dimble saying her prayers, was too wide. These things belonged, for her, to different worlds. On the one hand, terror of dreams, rapture of obedience, the tingling light and sound from under the Director's door, and the great struggle against an imminent danger; on the other, the smell of pews, horrible lithographs of the Saviour (apparently seven feet high, with the face of a consumptive girl), the embarrassment of confirmation classes, the nervous affability of clergymen. . . . It now appeared that almost anything might be true. . . . Maleldil might be, quite simply and crudely, God. (234)

Here Lewis's "smuggled theology" is brought out into the clear light of day. Some critics find his thematic strategy ingenious and exhilarating, while others reject this technique as itself simple and crude.[22]

By the time readers finish the trilogy, they have visited two other worlds, encountered creatures natural and preternatural, and witnessed a hnakra hunt, a fatal shooting, hand-to-hand combat, and finally mass destruction. Amid all these goings-on, readers have also had reiterated for them Christian teachings on creation, the revolt of Lucifer, the fall of Adam and Eve, the Incarnation, plus an intimation of the Last Judgment. One may argue about Lewis's admixture of narration and exposition or decry his tendency to reduce complex philosophical and sociological issues to a battle between Light and Darkness. But in the end one cannot help but admit the resourcefulness and conviction with which Lewis weaves his worldview into the fabric of his fiction.

3

The Recovered Image: Elements of Classicism and Medievalism

> *Humanity does not pass through phases as a train passes through stations: being alive, it has the privilege of always moving yet never leaving anything behind. Whatever we have been, in some sort we still are.*
>
> C. S. Lewis, *The Allegory of Love*

It is not surprising that the theological orientation of the trilogy is distinctly medieval in character. Lewis's whole person was drawn to a time when Western civilization could with some accuracy be called Christendom and when a predominant literary form was epic romance. The world of Aquinas and of King Arthur, of Boethius and Boiardo, was the world in which Lewis the scholar, the Christian, and the lover of heroic adventure could feel most at home. In his scholarly works such as *The Allegory of Love* and *The Discarded Image,* Lewis deftly elucidates a world-picture that has been set aside for centuries; in the trilogy he seeks to recover that image for modern readers.

The usual paradigm, still found in many history books, is that ancient Greece and Rome achieved the first apex in Western civilization—the classical era. Then came a hiatus lasting for centuries, the so-called Dark Ages and Middle Ages. (Even the term "medieval" means nothing more than "middle era.") Finally, the cultural stagnation was overcome by the humanists, who awakened a slumbering glory and began the ascent to a new cultural apex.

Lewis found this common view of Western civilization presumptuous and misleading. He anticipated contemporary post-structuralist historiography by noting that historical events are not self-interpreting; facts must be "read" according to some set of presuppositions, whether acknowledged or unacknowledged. Thus, in his inaugural address as professor of medieval and Renaissance literature at Cambridge, Lewis quoted G. M. Trevelyan approvingly: "Unlike dates, periods are not facts. They are retrospective conceptions that we form about past events, useful to focus discussion, but very often leading historical thought astray" (*SLE* 2).

Lewis went on to argue that historical thought has indeed been led astray by the stratification of Western cultural history into classical, medieval, and Renaissance periods. He denied that the medieval era represented a radical break with the classical era, or that the Renaissance represented a radical break with the Middle Ages. The real break, he argued, came in the intellectual revolution of the nineteenth and twentieth centuries, which separates the modern world from previous eras much more than any of them are separated from each other.

Rather than accepting a fundamental shift between the classical world and the Christian era, Lewis consistently stressed the continuity between the pagan and the Christian. In *The Discarded Image,* for example, he spends two pages showing that pagans and early Christians had far more in common than either shares with the modern Zeitgeist. He concludes that "the modern who dislikes the Christian Fathers would have disliked the Pagan philosophers equally, and for similar reasons" (47).

Pagan is another word that has a specialized meaning and private connotations in the Lewis lexicon. In common parlance, *pagan* and *Christian* are practically antonyms, the first representing a secular, this-worldly attitude, and the second representing its opposite. Lewis saw no such antithesis; he called paganism "the childhood of religion . . . a prophetic dream" (*SBJ* 235). For him, paganism was an anticipation, Christianity the fulfillment. He elaborated his view in a letter to Dom Bede Griffiths, his former student: "Paganism does not merely survive but first becomes really itself in the very heart of Christianity. By the way, would you agree that the un-

Christening of Europe (much of it) is an even bigger change than its Christening? So that the gap between Professor Ryle [a behaviorist philosopher] and say Dante, is *wider* than that between Dante and Virgil?" (*LCSL* 258). As can be seen here, Lewis defined paganism according to the masters of antiquity—Homer, Plato, and Virgil—not with the self-conscious neopaganism of a Swinburne or a Wilde.

In so defining his terms, Lewis is revealing personal history as well as his reading of cultural history. He associated paganism with myth and romance, and Christianity with the reality that myth and romance point to. Just as his own love of myth and romance was fulfilled when he reaffirmed his childhood faith, he saw the highest strivings of paganism fulfilled with the coming of the Christian era. Soon after his reconversion, Lewis speculated to Arthur Greeves: "I think the thrill of the Pagan stories and of romance may be due to the fact that they are mere beginnings—the first, faint whisper of the wind from beyond the world—while Christianity is the thing itself" (*TST* 430). It becomes clear in this context that when Lewis refers to himself in *Surprised by Joy* as "a converted Pagan living among apostate Puritans" (69), he is not referring to some militant secularism or riotous living in his early years, but rather to his acute responsiveness to "the whisper of the wind from beyond the world."

Just as he stressed the continuity between the classical and the Christian, Lewis also stressed the continuity between the medieval era and the Renaissance. He described the notion of the "medieval" as a fifteenth-century humanistic invention that dismissed "a thousand years of theology, metaphysics, jurisprudence, courtesy, poetry, and architecture . . . as a mere gap, chasm, or *enter-acte*" (*EL* 20). He also avoided the term *Renaissance* because he considered it an empty term of self-congratulation invented by the same humanists, one that imposed an illusory unity upon a heterogeneous assortment of cultural events (*EL* 55). Lewis's view is best summed up by his oft-quoted remark that "the Renaissance never happened in England; . . . if it did, it had no importance."[1] The influence of Lewis's revisionist reading of Western culture was already apparent in his lifetime, when Magdalene College, Cambridge, created for him the position of professor of medieval and Renaissance literature. In accepting the position, Lewis applauded the title "Medieval *and* Renaissance," asserting that "the barrier between those two ages has been greatly exaggerated, if indeed it was not largely a figment of Humanist propaganda" (*SLE* 2).

Here again we find interesting correlations between Lewis's reading of cultural history and his reading of his own life. In his discussion of the humanists, he seems to associate them with his traumatic memories of the years he spent in the public schools. He speaks of the "schoolroom severities" (*EL* 21) of the humanists and comments on their strictures concerning syntax and grammar by explaining, "You must not do in English things you were whipped at school for doing in Latin" (22). Lewis also compares the humanists' emulation of the classics to a "desire to be very 'adult' " (24). And when Lewis asserts that the humanists created "a new literary quality—vulgarity" (24), we cannot help but think of his portrait of himself as a schoolboy aping the foppish older lads, and concluding, "a new element entered my life: vulgarity" (*SBJ* 67).

Lewis devoted a great deal of his energy and expertise as a scholar to the task of rehabilitating the medieval worldview, urging his readers to recognize the intellectual and artistic achievements of writers who might otherwise have been considered mainly as precursors. For example, he reiterated in several published works that medieval authors knew the earth to be a globe and that they thought of it as a very small point in comparison to the vastness of the universe (*EL* 2; *Mir* 50; *SMRL* 46–47). (One of the authors whom Lewis faulted for perpetuating the myth of medieval ignorance on these matters was J. B. S. Haldane [*DI* 97].)

Out of the Silent Planet

When Lewis turned his hand to fiction, his task was not to argue for the intellectual vitality of the medieval worldview but rather to show its imaginative beauty. Throughout the Ransom trilogy Lewis tries to suggest, through the vehicle of space fantasy, what the medieval vision of reality might have felt like from "inside."

Early in *Out of the Silent Planet* Lewis serves notice that he does not intend to follow the usual genre conventions about cosmic voyages. While his reading of Wells and others as a boy had impressed upon him the "vastness and cold of space" (*SBJ* 65), his own protagonist discovers just the opposite. Having been drugged by Weston and Devine and hauled toward their spacecraft, Ransom awakens to an invigorating "tyranny of heat and light," which surprises him, since he had expected space to be dark and cold (*OSP* 29). In describing what Ransom feels when gazing at the cosmos from the side of the spacecraft away from the sun, Lewis enthralls the reader with some of the most evocative prose to be found in the trilogy.

> The Earth's disk was nowhere to be seen; the stars, thick as daisies on an uncut lawn, reigned perpetually with no cloud, no moon, no sunrise to dispute their sway. There were planets of unbelievable majesty, and constellations undreamed of: there were celestial sapphires, rubies, emeralds and pin-pricks of burning gold; far out on the left of the picture hung a comet, tiny and remote; and between all and behind all, far more emphatic and palpable than it showed on Earth, the undimensioned, enigmatic blackness. The lights trembled: they seemed to grow brighter as he looked. Stretched naked on his bed, a second Danaë, he found it night by night more difficult to disbelieve in old astrology: almost he felt, wholly he imagined, "sweet influence" pouring or even stabbing into his surrendered body. (31)

Kath Filmer has pointed out how Lewis's choice of metaphors in this passage underscores his attraction to a hierarchical worldview. Quoting Robbe-Grillet's dictum that "metaphor is never an innocent figure of speech," Filmer notes that readers are invited to see the beauty of the scene in terms of earthly monarchs reigning in serene and undisputed majesty.[2] The references to precious stones and to a comet hanging in space like a rich tapestry also suggest a regal setting.

In referring to "sweet influence" and to Danaë, Lewis carries the process a step further. Throughout the trilogy he treats the old astrology and the old mythology as vestiges of lost realities. Our word *influence* derives from astrology, from the belief that a force emanating from celestial bodies "flows into" humans, influencing their behavior.

As well as imagining he can actually feel this force, Ransom also identifies with Danaë, the woman whom Zeus ravished in the form of a shower of gold. Lewis admired a cycle of poems on Danaë appearing in Robert Nichols's volume of poetry *Ardours and Endurances* (*TST* 235). These poems portray her as the infatuated lover of Zeus, breathlessly awaiting his visitation. Something of this same sense of enraptured surrender is suggested in Ransom's willing exposure to the celestial radiance.

As the voyage toward Malacandra continues, Ransom comes to consider the very term *space* a serious misnomer.

> But Ransom, as time wore on, became aware of another and more spiritual cause for his progressive lightening and exultation of heart. A nightmare, long engendered in the modern mind by the mythology that follows in the wake of science, was falling off him. He had read of "Space": at the back of his thinking for years had lurked the dismal fancy of the black, cold vacuity, the utter deadness, which was supposed to separate the worlds. He had not known how much it affected him till now—now the very name "Space" seemed a blasphemous libel for this empyrean ocean of radiance in which they swam. He could not call it "dead"; he felt life pouring into him from it every moment. . . . No: Space was the wrong name. Older thinkers had been wiser when they named it simply the heavens—the heavens which declared the glory—the
>
> "happy climes that ly
> Where day never shuts his eye
> Up in the broad fields of the sky." (*OSP* 32)

Here again Lewis's description invites the reader to set aside the "mythology which follows in the wake of science" and to reconsider older mythologies, echoed in Milton's realm of unblinking day (*Comus,* lines 976–78) and the psalmist's heavens that declare God's glory (Ps. 19:1).

Lewis would not have been greatly disturbed to learn that actual travelers into space would find more the "black, cold vacuity" than the "empyrean oceans of radiance" he envisioned. He had little interest in the scientific side of science fiction. When he wrote *Out of the Silent Planet,* he knew that there were no actual canals on Mars, and he confessed that Weston's "scientific" explanation of how his spacecraft flew was "pure mumbo jumbo" (*OOW* 76, 87). He used the fantasy genre not to depict the universe as understood in our century but to re-create imaginatively the medieval cosmology, a vast and magnificent picture that Lewis called "the greatest work of art the Middle Ages produced" (*SMRL* 62).

Descriptive passages like those quoted above frequently parallel Lewis's remarks about medieval cosmology in his scholarly works. For example, his essay "Imagination and Thought in the Middle Ages" is intended as an introduction to the medieval world picture but serves equally well as a gloss on *Out of the Silent Planet.* In this essay he explains that when people in the Middle Ages gazed up at a night sky, they did not think of the spaces they looked at as silent, dark, or empty (*SMRL* 52). He also discusses the medieval understanding of "influences" (56) and quotes the same passage from *Comus* that Ransom had recalled so fondly (53).

In *The Discarded Image* Lewis again underscores the differences between the ancients' picture of the heavens and our perception of outer space. He quotes the Latin poet Lucan, who envisions celestial realms bathed in light: "How dark, compared with the aether, our terrestrial day is" (*DI* 33). He also contrasts the medieval and the modern in language similar to the passage from *Out of the Silent Planet* quoted above: "Nothing is more deeply impressed on the cosmic imaginings of a modern than the idea that the heavenly bodies move in a pitch-black and dead-cold vacuity. It was not so in the Medieval Model" (*DI* 111).

Apart from reimagining "space" according to the medieval model, Lewis also redefines the planets that float in space. When Ransom and his abductors approach Malacandra, they experience nausea, headaches, and heart palpitations (*OSP* 38). At first one may consider this merely Lewis's (fairly accurate) predictions about the physiological effects of moving from a weightless state back into a gravity field. But soon it becomes clear that he has something more in mind. As the spacecraft descends, Ransom again finds his former conceptions reversed.

> Suddenly the lights of the Universe seemed to be turned down. As if some demon had rubbed the heaven's face with a dirty sponge, the splendour in which they had lived for so long blenched to a pallid, cheerless and pitiable grey. . . . What had been a chariot gliding in the fields of heaven became a dark steel box dimly lighted by a slit of window, and falling. They were falling out of the heaven, into a world. . . . He wondered how he could ever have thought of planets, even of the Earth, as islands of life and reality floating in a deadly void. Now, with a certainty which never after deserted him, he saw the planets—the "earths" he had called them in his thought—as mere holes or gaps in the living heaven—excluded and rejected wastes of heavy matter and murky air, formed not by addition to, but by subtraction from, the surrounding brightness. (*OSP* 39–40)

In general, Lewis presents life on Malacandra as very positive, even utopian, so many readers are puzzled to find him describing Ransom's entry into this world in such negative terms. The passage quoted above seems neither "scientific" nor thematically congruent with the rest of the book. Yet again the explanation can be found in Lewis's own discussion of medieval cosmology. In *The Discarded Image,* he explains the hierarchy of created substance developed by the fifth-century author Macrobius: ether, the purest and most limpid form, rose the highest; beneath it came air, less pure and more heavy; then came water, and finally solids. As Lewis sums up: "Finally out of the whole tumult of matter all that was irreclaimable (*vastum*) was scraped off and cleansed from the (other) elements (*ex defaecatis abrasum elementis*) and sank down and settled at the lowest point, plunged in binding and unending cold. Earth is in fact the 'offscourings of creation,' the cosmic dustbin" (*DI* 62–63). According to this order of creation, any planet, even an "unfallen" one, cannot match the glory and spendor of the heavens themselves.

Yet if one must inhabit a world, Malacandra turns out to be a very good choice. Weston and Devine, thinking they have come to offer Ransom as a human sacrifice to the inhabitants of Malacandra, have severely misunderstood the beings they have encountered there. Once Ransom escapes his abductors and meets the three rational species on the planet—the hrossa, the seroni, and the pfifltriggi—he discovers what he had least been expecting: a utopian society. In fact, *Out of the Silent Planet* has been interpreted both as an answer to Plato's *Republic* and as an answer to Wells's utopian novels.[3]

Writers of utopian fiction generally present societies where the author's own cherished ideals have been successfully implemented. Lewis is no exception to this rule: the Malacandrian society he portrays as so attractive is a relatively simple society of hunter/poets, shepherd/philosophers, and artisans. As Ransom comes to know the inhabitants of that world, he learns their ideas about love, art, and spirituality—ideas usually similar to Lewis's own opinions on these subjects. Malacandrian society is also hierarchical, even theocratic, as well as preindustrial and precapitalistic. In short, it approaches the medieval ideal of a well-governed Christian society.

For example, when Ransom recounts the sordid history of earth to a gathering of sorns, they interpret our planet's woes in terms of a breakdown in the Great Chain of Being: "There must be rule, yet how can creatures rule themselves? Beasts must be ruled by *hnau* and *hnau* by *eldila* and *eldila* by Maleldil" (*OSP* 102). (As shown in chapter 2 this formulation may be translated to mean that beasts must be ruled by rational species, rational species by angels, and angels by God.)

In *A Preface to Paradise Lost* Lewis argues that "the Hierarchical conception" dominated Western conceptions of order—cosmic, political, and moral—from Aristotle to Milton. With God at the top of the great chain and unformed matter at the bottom, everyone and everything had a natural station, ruling over those below, obeying those above. A great many sins, according to this conception, derive from not recognizing one's station, and thus perverting the natural order. In Lewis's reading of Milton, Lucifer sins by rebelling against his natural superiors, while Adam sins by not ruling over his natural subject, Eve.

It is not hard to see that Lewis had a great deal of imaginative sympathy for this view of the cosmic order. In the Ransom trilogy, he pictures a cosmos ordered hierarchically, with only "the silent planet," earth, out of harmony with the natural order. In the Narnia chronicles as well, Lewis portrays the ideal society as a monarchy;

those who advocate self-rule in the chronicles are not portrayed as reformers or democrats, but as self-interested demagogues or sullen and insubordinate subjects. Lewis was pragmatic enough to advocate democracy for the contemporary world—not because people are good enough to deserve it, but because they are so prone to abuse power that it needs to be spread out (*OOW* 81). Nonetheless, democracy seemed to him, like so much else about the contemporary world, prosaic and utilitarian, compared to the grandeur and elegance of earlier eras.

Having woven medieval motifs into *Out of the Silent Planet,* Lewis reveals at the end of the story that his own work as a medievalist led him to discover the extraordinary adventures of Elwin Ransom on Malacandra. In chapter 22, Lewis says that he will dispense with literary conventions, drop the mask, and tell his real purpose for writing the book (*OSP* 152). In claiming to abandon the mask of fiction, Lewis thus offers his readers an even more ingenious fiction than the one they have been reading.

At this point, Lewis the author becomes a character in his own story. He explains that he learned of Ransom's voyage after writing to him about the curious word *Oyarses,* which Lewis had run across in the work of Bernardus Silvestris, a twelfth-century Platonist. Another scholar, identified only as C. J., had interpreted the term as a corruption of *ousiarches,* a ruler of a heavenly sphere, or tutelary spirit of a planet. Ransom replied to Lewis's query by inviting him to come over for the weekend, so Ransom could relate his adventures on Malacandra. He felt compelled to do so to convince Lewis that *Oyarsa* was not just a philological oddity but an actual being, a powerful one, known to the ancients but now forgotten on "the silent planet." Ransom convinces Lewis to write up Ransom's cosmic voyage in the form of fiction, arguing that it would be more advantageous to appeal to readers' imaginations than to attack their intellectual presuppositions directly. Ransom explains to the narrator that "what we need for the moment is not so much a body of belief as a body of people familiarized with certain ideas. If we could even effect in one per cent of our readers a change-over from the conception of Space to the conception of Heaven, we should have made a beginning" (*OSP* 154). Here we see Lewis at once being perfectly candid and perfectly crafty. Of course, he did not really expect readers to believe in a literal Ransom who really had traveled to Mars (though he did receive a number of letters asking if all this had actually happened [*LCSL* 261]). But he really does hope to "baptize the imagination" of his readers, to make them wonder if there are not indeed unseen realities not accounted for by the modern, materialistic worldview. Lewis really is dropping his mask and speaking with sincere conviction when he warns readers of dangers that "are not planetary but cosmic, . . . not temporal but eternal" (*OSP* 153).

Throughout the trilogy, Lewis maintains this strategy of intermixing his fictional world with our "factual" world. Besides using himself as character, Lewis's references to the obscure term *Oyarses,* to Bernardus Silvestris, and even to "C. J." are all taken from "real life." Lewis discusses Bernardus Silvestris at length in *The Allegory of Love* (90–98), where he offers the theory of Prof. C. C. J. Webb that *Oyarses* is a corruption of the Greek *Ousiarches* (362). Here again, as so often in Lewis's books, the ideas discussed in his expository works are given an imaginative embodiment in his fiction.

Perelandra

Near the end of *Out of the Silent Planet,* Ransom speaks of having "made a beginning" in re-forming readers' imaginations, and Lewis promises his readers another story (154). *Perelandra* takes up where *Out of the Silent Planet* left off, not only in its use of medieval motifs, but also in its strategy of intermixing Lewis's fictional world with our factual world.

In the second book of the trilogy Lewis again presents himself as a character in the story, and again he refers to an obscure medieval scholar, one who knows more about spiritual beings than his supposedly more sophisticated modern counterparts. In describing his encounter with an eldil at Ransom's cottage, Lewis adds a footnote quoting Natvilcius, who seems to know a great deal about angels, even speculating about their actual, celestial bodies in contrast to the way they are perceived by human eyes. Lewis scholars have searched his other books and pored over many a reference source trying to discover the identity of this Natvilcius. Unable to find any references to him outside of *Perelandra,* some modestly conclude that they do not know if he really existed or not, while others go on record as assuming that Natvilcius is one of Lewis's own inventions.[4]

This second, bolder group of Lewis scholars is correct. Sometimes when Lewis chose to write anonymously, he used the letters "N.W." Most of his occasional poems were published with these initials, and the first edition of *A Grief Observed* appeared with "N. W. Clerk" as its author. "N.W." is short for *Nat Whilk,* Old English for "I know not whom." It is the archaic equivalent of the modern phrase "author unknown."

Natvilcius is simply the latinized form of "Nat Whilk." Unlike his reference to the actual author Bernardus Silvestris in *Out of the Silent Planet,* Lewis has created here a fictional scholar to introduce his idea that eldils exist on a celestial plane and can be perceived only imperfectly by creatures confined to three-dimensional space. Even Lewis's little hoax here is an oblique tribute to a medieval author. In his essay "What Chaucer Did to 'Il Filostrato,'" Lewis notes with seeming delight Chaucer's citation of fictitious sources to lend a greater sense of historicity to *Troilus and Cressida* (*SLE* 30).

Once Ransom reaches Perelandra, he finds that, like Malacandra, it is a hierarchical world ruled by a king and queen. Though these are the first pair, as yet without descendants, they rule the animals and will eventually have authority over the Oyarsa of this world as well. Ransom is confused by this seeming reversal of the cosmic order, but the queen explains to him their world was created after Maleldil the Younger had taken human form. As unfallen humans the king and queen need have no authorities between themselves and Maleldil.

Though it might seem grievous for eldils to serve those whom they once ruled, the queen explains that it is "their glory and their joy" to nurture creatures before whom they would later bow (82–83). Later the Oyarsa of Perelandra confirms this, saying that her relationship with the royal pair is like that of two Perelandran creatures, the dumb dam who suckles the singing beast: "The [singing beasts] have no milk and always what they bring forth is suckled by the she-beast of another kind. She is great and beautiful and dumb, and till the young singing beast is weaned it is among her whelps and is subject to her. But when it is grown it becomes the most delicate and glorious of all beasts and goes from her. And she wonders at its song" (196). In this passage Lewis suggests that a hierarchical social order entails more complex relationships than usually understood in our era, when the only political models we are familiar with are democratic, autocratic, or totalitarian.

Lewis often referred to the medieval metaphor of the dance, both as an image of their social order and their concept of the cosmic order. In *Miracles* he explains that hierarchy itself is more like a dance than a pyramid.

> The partner who bows to Man in one movement of the dance receives Man's reverences in another. To be high or central means to abdicate continually: to be low means to be raised: all good masters are servants: God washes the feet of men. The concepts we usually bring to the consideration of such matters are miserably political and prosaic. We think of flat repetitive equality and arbitrary privilege as the only two alternatives—thus missing all the overtones, the counterpoint, the vibrant sensitiveness, the inter-inanimations of reality. (128)

This is a highly idealized version of hierarchy, one that could succeed only in unfallen worlds. Yet it does show how closely interwoven were Lewis's theological convictions and his love of medievalism. Just after the passage from *Miracles* quoted above, Lewis calls the principle of descent and reascent "the very formula of reality" (129). God had to descend into human form in order to redeem humanity; Christ had to descend into earth and then reascend three days later in order to complete his atoning work; humans must likewise descend into earth before they are raised up again on some final day.

In this context, it is interesting to recall that Ransom is carried to Perelandra in a casket, which descends and then reascends upon plunging into the seas of Perelandra (34). Later, when he is dragged downward to the ocean's depths by the Un-man, the language describing his descent (171–72) is intriguingly similar to the language Lewis uses in *Miracles,* in which he compares the Incarnation to the descent and reascent of a deep-sea diver (116).

Behind Lewis's principle of ascent and reascent and his metaphors taken from dancing is the medieval commonplace of the Great Dance. Though we have become accustomed since Newton's time to think of the universe as essentially a mechanism, the medieval picture was much more festive. Lewis noted in one of his lectures on medieval cosmologists that their symbol for the primum mobile was a young girl dancing and playing a tambourine. He explains that the orderly movements of the heavenly spheres in the medieval picture "are to be conceived not as those of a machine or even an army, but rather as a dance, a festival, a symphony, a ritual, a carnival, or all of these in one" (*SMRL* 60).

The Great Dance in the closing pages of *Perelandra* summarizes a great deal of theology in poetic form, as well as imaginatively recapturing some of the medieval sense of festival, symphony, ritual, and carnival. As Roland M. Kawano has observed, a central element in the image of the dance is "the reconciliation of order and freedom."[5] In the dance, beasts, humans and spirits all find their place; fallen worlds and unfallen ones, ancient ones and new ones, each participate in the pageant.

The dance also serves as a kind of liturgical answer to the angst produced by positivism, the sense that humans inhabit a vast, dead universe that mocks all philosophy, all desire for justice, all yearning for some larger meaning. As Ransom chased the Weston/Un-man over seemingly illimitable seas, he became overwhelmed by "mere bigness and loneliness" and felt that those vast solitudes were haunted, not by some god, but by "the wholly inscrutable to which man and his life remained eternally irrelevant" (164). Thinking of the even vaster solitudes of space, Ransom was oppressed by what he calls the Empirical Bogey, "the great myth of our century with its gases and galaxies, its light years and evolutions, its nightmare perspectives of simple arithmetic in which everything that can possibly hold significance for the mind becomes the mere by-product of essential disorder" (164). Once Ransom caught up with the Un-man, the Weston-voice echoed many of Ransom's own anxieties about some fundamental meaninglessness at the core of things (167–69). At the time Ransom had nothing to recommend except to repent and offer a child's prayer.

But the Great Dance offers a whole different cosmic picture. One speaker in the ritual affirms that Maleldil's greatness does not reside in "years to years in lumpish aggregations, or miles to miles and galaxies to galaxies" (214); for all of him dwells in the seed of the smallest flower and is not cramped, yet "Deep Heaven is inside Him who is inside the seed and does not distend Him" (215). Another voice explains that in the Great Dance all is at the center, whether the dust or beasts or hnau species or gods, for "where Maleldil is, there is the center" (216). A third voice, most directly addressing the Empirical Bogey, proclaims, "All that is made seems planless to the darkened mind, because there are more plans than it looked for. . . . There seems no plan because it is all plan: there seems no centre because it is all centre" (218).

Lewis, the medieval scholar, would revel in such a glad, elegant, and orderly picture of the cosmos. Lewis the twentieth-century Christian would admit that such a picture was not scientifically true, but he affirmed that its theological implications were essentially accurate.

That Hideous Strength

In the first two books of the trilogy, Ransom traveled to other worlds to discover the truth of myth and to find a cosmos more similar to medieval models than to modern ones. In *That Hideous Strength* Arthurian legend and other medieval traditions prove their relevance, and reality, on twentieth-century earth.

The most prominent Arthurian element in the third novel of the trilogy is the return of Merlin. Bragdon Wood, the ancient garden owned by Bracton College, is the site of Merlin's Well, the reputed resting place of Arthur's wizard. The leaders of N.I.C.E, those who know its real goals, would like to unearth Merlin and awaken him from his enchanted slumber in order to combine his powers with their own.

It might seem highly incongruous to have modern technocrats trying to use magic, but in *The Abolition of Man* Lewis argues that science and magic spring from the same impulse.

> There was very little magic in the Middle Ages: the sixteenth and seventeenth centuries are the high noon of magic. The serious magical endeavour and the serious scientific endeavour are twins: one was sickly and died, the other strong and throve. . . . There is something which unites magic and applied science while separating both from the "wisdom" of earlier ages. For the wise men of old the cardinal problem had been how to conform the soul to reality, and the solution had been knowledge, self-discipline, and virtue. For magic and applied science alike the problem is how to subdue reality to the wishes of men. (87–88)

Since Lewis identifies magic not with the Middle Ages but with the humanists who came afterward, one can see why the words *magic* and *magician* usually have negative connotations in his writings. Magicians in Lewis's fiction (see *The Magician's Nephew*) and his nonfiction are generally depicted as those who abrogate moral laws in order to gain illicit power over nature and over others. Even in *That Hideous Strength* Lewis takes pains to distinguish Merlin's kind of magic, which originated in Atlantis, from Renaissance magic (201).

Once Merlin is awakened from fifteen centuries of sleep, he does not unite his powers with N.I.C.E. but joins the humble company at St. Anne's. Eventually he becomes the instrument by which the conspirators at N.I.C.E. are exterminated. This resolution to the story has troubled some critics. Chad Walsh, for example, complains that Merlin's role in the story comes close to being a deus ex machina and that the victory of Ransom and his followers is based upon the lucky circumstance that they found Merlin before the others did.[6] But this objection overlooks several key elements in the narrative. First, Merlin does not simply stumble into the hands of the good side. Once he awakens, he is guided by some preternatural means, and he rides directly to St. Anne's and Ransom. Second, Merlin does not offer his services to whoever asks. He subjects Ransom to three arcane questions that no one at N.I.C.E. could have possibly answered (272–74). Ransom can speak to these occult matters because he has traveled to other worlds and continues to have contact with lords of other planets. In their conversation, Ransom learns that Merlin, despite his rather druidic appearance, is a Christian—another reason Merlin would never have allied himself with N.I.C.E. Finally, it should be noted that Merlin does not destroy Belbury using his own weapons alone. Ransom arranges to have the powers of the Oyarsas channeled into Merlin (317), powers that the leaders of N.I.C.E. could not have drawn upon.

Merlin submits to Ransom's authority, not just because Ransom can answer Merlin's questions, but because Ransom is the pendragon. In Arthurian tradition, the pendragon is the head of all the armies in times of war. Though Arthur was only one of many kings in his time, he inherited the title of pendragon from his father, Uther, so he was the chief commander in the wars against the Anglo-Saxons. (Pendragon is from Celtic "head of a dragon," taken from the dragon's head pictured on the standard of the one who held the title.) Lewis imagines that the title has been passed down secretly from generation to generation and that it now rests upon the one appointed to lead the battle against a new type of invasion. As pendragon, Ransom is also the head of Logres. From the Welsh word for "England," Logres traditionally represents the Britain of King Arthur, whose royal court was at Camelot. Though Logres is mentioned in Spenser and Milton with about the same connotations as the word "Camelot," Lewis's friend Charles Williams gave the term a more specialized meaning. In his Arthurian books, Williams used Logres to represent the spiritual side of England, the combination of Christian and Celtic ideals, a force that stands against the tides of worldliness and corruption.

Lewis adopted this usage in *That Hideous Strength,* as seen in Professor Dimble's outline of English history: "Something we may call Britain is always haunted by something we may call Logres. Haven't you noticed that we are two countries? After every Arthur, a

Mordred; behind every Milton, a Cromwell: a nation of poets, a nation of shopkeepers; the home of Sidney—and of Cecil Rhodes. Is it any wonder they call us hypocrites? But what they mistake for hypocrisy is really the struggle between Logres and Britain" (369). Lewis's likes and dislikes are certainly made evident here. Mordred is Arthur's nephew (or bastard son in some versions) who betrayed Arthur and brought an end to Camelot. Milton and Cromwell represent the best and the worst of Puritanism. (As an Ulsterman by birth, Lewis resented Cromwell's brutal suppression of the Irish.)[7] Sir Philip Sidney is Lewis's ideal of the poet-statesman, while Cecil Rhodes was the architect of Britain's imperialistic and exploitative policies in the African country that once bore his name.

Besides his title of pendragon, Ransom is also called Mr. Fisher-King. Lewis offers a rather contrived explanation for this, noting that Ransom received a large inheritance from his sister, Mrs. Fisher-King, on the condition that he take her name (114). Despite this unconvincing detail, the name does add another Arthurian dimension to the story and to Ransom's role in it. In the matter of Britain, the fisher-king is the keeper of the grail, a fisherman and king wounded in the thighs who holds court at his castle, Carbonek. The knight-errant Percival (or Parsifal) visits the grail castle and finds the fisher-king in pain, reclining on a couch in front of a fire. During dinner Percival sees a bleeding lance and a radiant golden cup but does not ask about them. The next morning he learns that his fateful silence has serious consequences: the fisher-king cannot be healed, and all his lands will be devastated. This is the beginning of Percival's quest to recover the grail. There are different versions of what happens to Percival. Some versions end happily, some not so. But all present the fisher-king as a wounded godlike figure who is keeper of the grail.

Ellen Rawson has shown that Jane Studdock is a new Percival in *That Hideous Strength.* When Jane first visits Ransom, his chamber seems to her like a throne room, and she finds him reclining in front of a fire with a painful wound, just as the fisher-king appeared to Percival. Ransom reminds her of King Arthur and of Solomon, and for the first time since childhood she could "taste the word *King* itself with all linked associations of battle, marriage, priesthood, mercy, and power" (*THS* 143). Percival became a Christian because of his encounter with the fisher-king, who is a Christ-figure in most versions of the grail legend. Jane too discovers spiritual realities at St. Anne's, coming to suspect that Maleldil is indeed God (234) and finally surrendering her will to Maleldil's (318–19).

Besides his roles as pendragon and fisher-king, Ransom embodies other Arthurian elements as well. In answer to one of Merlin's questions, Ransom explains that King Arthur is not dead but sits in the House of Kings in the land of Abhalljin on Perelandra (274). Later it is revealed that Ransom will be taken to Perelandra to be with Arthur once his work on earth is done. Abhalljin (spelled "Aphallin" on page 368) is taken from the Welsh term *Afallon,* the abode of dead heroes, the Celtic version of Elysium. In Arthurian legend this appears as "Avalon," the mystic isle where Arthur is taken to be healed of his wounds. Since the trilogy suggests that Perelandra is the true source of all myths of paradise, it is only fitting that Avalon should be found there and that Ransom should be healed on the world where he was wounded.

At the end of *That Hideous Strength* Venus herself (the Oyarsa of Perelandra) descends to earth not only to carry Ransom back to her world but also to unite with the other Oyeresu in defeating the dark powers that have gathered at N.I.C.E. Ransom had discovered the reality of planetary "influences" when he traveled through the heavens to Malacandra, though astrology plays only an incidental role in *Out of the Silent Planet.* But in *That Hideous Strength,* all of the planetary intelligences meet with Ransom and Merlin, their very proximity making the rest of the company at St. Anne's successively mercurial, amorous, martial, saturnine, and jovial. This chapter, "The Descent of the Gods," is a brilliant prose-poem on how planetary influence might be supposed to affect human psyches, but it also sets up the turning point in the story: the passing of their powers into Merlin for the purpose of eradicating N.I.C.E.

Astrology is associated with St. Anne's just as clearly as magic is associated with Belbury. Since Lewis did not approve of magic, one supposes at first that he would not have any imaginative attraction for astrology either. But Lewis explains in his volume of the *Oxford History of English Literature* that magic and astrology were never allied. While the first occult science sought power over nature, the second assumed nature's power over humans (*EL* 6). Lewis also noted that medieval astrologers did not believe that the planets compelled human behavior, only influenced it. The usual view in the Middle Ages, he says, was that a person, assisted by grace, could overcome a bad horoscope just as he or she could overcome a naturally bad temper (*SMRL* 55).

Apart from Arthurian and astrological elements, another medieval motif that figures prominently in *That Hideous Strength* is the image of the enclosed garden. In the Song of Solomon and other books of the Old Testament, the walled garden is a protected place, associated most often with a woman's virginity. In the Middle Ages, the walled garden symbol accrued multiple associations. As Lewis explains in *The Allegory of Love,* the enclosed garden is associated with youth and youthful love in early writers like Andreas Capellanus and Claudius; in Guillaume de Lorris, it includes also the life of the court, the arena for games of love; in later writers it represents allegorically the heart of a woman and the many emotions that reside there. "Deeper than these," concludes Lewis, "lies the world-wide dream of the happy garden—the island of the Hesperides, the earthly paradise, Tirnanog" (119–20).

This summation is perfectly sound scholarship, but it also reveals the man behind the literary historian. The Garden of the Hesperides is the image of Joy, or *Sehnsucht,* that Lewis used most often—in *Surprised by Joy,* in *Perelandra,* and in his poetry. The phrase "the earthly paradise" is the title of a romance by William Morris, much beloved and often read by Lewis, which cleverly interweaves classical and medieval motifs. Tirnanog, "land of the young ones," is the Irish equivalent of Avalon.[8] Lewis most likely first heard of Tirnanog from his childhood nurse, Lizzie Endicott, who was full of Irish lore and song. So when Lewis speaks of the deeper meanings of garden imagery, he not only is casting light on the medieval mind but also is revealing his own. Besides the pictures of paradise he mentions, we might add Eden, Perelandra, and a toy garden on a biscuit tin.

In *That Hideous Strength* the sequestered garden first appears in the narrator's description of Bragdon Wood, the ancient copse owned by Bracton College and coveted by N.I.C.E. Indulging a bit too much in elaborate description and historical allusion, Lewis conjures up all the rich traditions of the place, going back to British-Roman times (i.e., the era of King Arthur). The narrator has a sense that he is penetrating a holy of holies as he enters Bragdon Wood (20), and this indeed will turn out to be a kind of sacred ground. After this elaborate spell of history and legend has been woven around Bragdon Wood by the narrator, readers cannot miss the irony when in the very next section of the novel, the bureaucrats at Bracton College treat this hallowed ground merely as a pink rectangle on a map, land to put up for sale.

While Mark Studdock and his colleagues are discussing what to do with Bragdon Wood, his wife, Jane, encounters another walled garden when she goes to visit Ransom and his little community at St. Anne's. As she is led toward the house, Jane passes by a vegetable garden and line of rosebushes that fill her with wistful thoughts: "It was a very large garden. It was like—like—yes, now she had it: it was like the garden in *Peter Rabbit.* Or was it like the garden in the *Romance of the Rose?* No, not in the least like really. Or like Klingsor's garden? Or the garden in *Alice?* Or like the garden on the top of some Mesopotamian ziggurat which had probably given rise to the whole legend of Paradise? Or simply like all walled gardens?" (61–62). The walled garden at St. Anne's evokes in Jane all those images of earthly paradise—from children's stories, to medieval romances, to ancient mythologies. The gardens of *Peter Rabbit* and *Alice's Adventures in Wonderland* are well known. *The Romance of the Rose* is an allegorical love poem begun in thirteenth-century France by Guillaume de Lorris and continued by Jean de Meung. It is discussed at length by Lewis in *The Allegory of Love;* indeed, Lewis's monumental work did a great deal to revive interest in the poem. All of these are enchanted gardens that evoke a sense of paradise.

Nancy Patterson associates "Klingsor's garden" with an exquisite garden described in "Klingsohr's Fairy Tale" by Novalis.[9] However, apart from the difference in spelling between "Klingsor" and

"Klingsohr," the garden in Novalis's story is a masterpiece of artifice, with metal trees and crystal flowers. It would seem a more fitting allusion to the garden at N.I.C.E. than at St. Anne's. A better identification, I believe, is the magic garden encountered by Parsifal when he approaches the castle of Klingsor, the magician in Wagner's *Parsifal* (1882). This is another allusion used by Lewis to link Jane with Percival and St. Anne's with the grail castle.

As she continues along the wall, Jane also ponders the sexual connotations of enclosed gardens, remembering Freud's theory that gardens were subliminal symbols of the female body. This reminder of her own unfulfilled sexuality and unhappy marriage changes her mood from one of reverie to one of defensiveness. As she approaches her first encounter with the now-transformed Ransom, she reminds herself that, at St. Anne's, she is on "hostile, or at least alien, ground" (62). But the hostility Jane senses is within her, not around her. She herself will be transformed by her increasing commitment to Maleldil's side.

Jane's husband, Mark, is transformed by the opposite process, by his nearly fatal entanglement with the dark forces who control N.I.C.E. In the closing pages of the novel, once Mark has recovered himself and realized how weary, flat, stale, and unprofitable all his ambitions have been, he discovers also that he really does love his estranged wife. At the same time Mark realizes that his lifelong obsession to be an insider has led him only to "the dry and choking places," he thinks of Jane as one who has within her "deep wells and knee-deep meadows of happiness, rivers of freshness, enchanted gardens of leisure, which he could not enter but could have spoiled" (247).

At the end of the story, Mark contemplates his failure as a husband and lover, and again he conjures up the image of the walled garden and the cloistered rose.

> All the lout and clown and clod-hopper in him was revealed to his own reluctant inspection; the coarse, male boor with horny hands and hobnailed shoes and beefsteak jaw . . . stumping in where great lovers, knights and poets, would have feared to tread. . . . [He] had behaved as if he were native to that fenced garden and even its

> natural possessor. . . . He was discovering the hedge after he had plucked the rose, and not only plucked it but torn it to pieces and crumpled it with hot, thumb-like, greedy fingers. (380–81)

Though Mark's mind is full of self-loathing here, he is actually gaining the humility and self-recognition needed to redeem him from moral failure. Remembering that there are no "innocent" metaphors, we sense that in using medieval motifs to describe Mark's thoughts, Lewis implies that Studdock is developing more humane patterns of thought and feeling.

Fortunately for Mark, one of the things that Jane has learned in her time at St. Anne's is forgiveness. So when Mark and Jane are reunited in a kind of honeymoon cottage, we feel assured that their marriage will be renewed. In a suitably medieval ending, it is Venus herself who bids Mark to go in to his wife and who blesses their marriage bed.

4

"Souls Who Have Lost the Intellectual Good": Portraits of Evil

> *The torture allotted to the Danaids in the classical underworld, that of attempting to fill sieves with water, is the symbol not of one vice but of all vices. It is the very mark of a perverse desire that it seeks what is not to be had.*
>
> C. S. Lewis, "The Inner Ring"

THE LAST BOOK of the Ransom trilogy represents the culmination of what might be termed the infernal period in Lewis's writings. In four consecutive books Lewis introduces hellish characters and hellish settings (imaginatively recast for modern readers) in order to explore the psychology of faith and doubt, of temptation and spiritual trial. In 1942 *The Screwtape Letters* appeared, featuring advice from a senior devil in the "lowerarchy" to a junior tempter. In 1943 came *Perelandra,* where Ransom spends half the story contending with a demonized corpse. In 1945 *That Hideous Strength* appeared, as well as *The Great Divorce,* a fantasy about denizens of hell who take an excursion to the outskirts of heaven, most finding reasons to prefer their nether abode.

Rooted as he was in traditional Christian doctrine and convinced of the theological soundness of much of the medieval worldview, Lewis believed in the reality of malevolent spirits opposed to God. But in the books mentioned above, the literal existence of the diabolical beings is secondary to their usefulness as metaphors of human vice and folly. Lewis believed that every moral choice humans make moves them one step closer to heaven or to hell; in fact, hell and heaven did not represent for him God's judgment so much as God's acknowledgment of the pattern of choices people make throughout their lifetimes. Lewis summed up his position best in *The Great Divorce:* "There are only two kinds of people in the end: those who say to God, 'Thy will be done,' and those to whom God says, in the end, '*Thy* will be done.' All that are in Hell, choose it" (72).

The villains in Lewis's fantasies are not hard to find; they do not, as Paul warned, cloak themselves as angels of light. Lewis's bad characters range from the merely pompous to the outright demonic, but they share a few common traits: they set aside ordinary morality in favor of utility or in favor of some lofty, abstract goals for humanity; they disregard the sanctity of life, whether human or animal; they are "progressive" and find little value in history, tradition, or the classics; they prefer the scientific, artificial, and industrial over the simple and natural; they use language to conceal and distort reality, rather than to reveal it. (Virtually all of these traits apply to the villains in the *Chronicles of Narnia* as well. Lewis's only work of fiction in which the major characters have a complex psychology, a mixture of good and bad traits, is *Till We Have Faces.* That is probably his only book that he would consider a novel in the strict sense of the term.)

No aspect of the trilogy has attracted more negative commentary than Lewis's portrayal of his bad characters. Let it be admitted at the outset that his villains are two-dimensional; most of them can be described in a single phrase, and they show no capacity for moral growth or change. Weston is a ruthless visionary; Devine is a cynical opportunist; Curry is a self-important string-puller; Hardcastle is a pitiless sadist. Virtually all of the personalities at N.I.C.E. could be described in such simple terms, and they all stay "in character" throughout *That Hideous Strength.* It is also clear that Lewis's good characters are generally associated with Christianity and with the humanities and that his evil characters are associated with modernism, in its various forms, and with the sciences.

Lewis's methods of characterization and his seeming antipathy to science are large issues that affect one's overall assessment of the trilogy. Concentrating on Lewis's villains in the trilogy, this chapter examines the banality of evil as Lewis understood it. Chapter 7 takes up the broader concerns of Lewis's attitude toward science and his success in delineating character.

Out of the Silent Planet

The first book of the trilogy opens with an atmosphere of subtle portent. Ransom walks alone under darkening skies between the towns of Sterk and Nadderby. The countryside along the road is described as desolate and featureless, and "more silent than an English landscape usually is" (8). *Sterk* is an earlier form of *stark;* it may also call to mind Starkness, the secret laboratory in the remote countryside where Maskull's adventures started in *Voyage to Arcturus.* Nadderby reminds us that the word *adder,* long a symbol of danger and intrigue, is formed by misdivision from the earlier word *nadder.*

When Ransom wriggles through the hedge at Weston and Devine's property, the sense of foreboding increases. The windows of the house are dark, and the path leading to the back of the house is rutted with the tracks of heavy lorry (truck) traffic. There is dense, factory-like smoke coming from somewhere in back. Since Lewis had an instinctive aversion to most things industrial, including factories and gas-powered vehicles, these may be taken as omens that something is amiss.

And something is amiss. When Ransom first stumbles across Weston and Devine struggling to subdue a simple-minded boy, Weston bellows, "May I ask who the devil you may be and what you are doing here?" Ransom mentions his promise to a poor woman, the boy's mother, but Devine interrupts: "Poor woman be damned" (12). And so it is throughout the trilogy. The characters whom Lewis called the "buffoon-villains" (*OOW* 77) constantly utter hellish oaths: "What the devil"; "Go to hell"; "That's infernal nonsense," and so forth. These characters reveal in their speech a state of mind that shows that Screwtape has them exactly where he wants them.

As they let the boy go, one of the two complains that they ought to have a dog to keep trespassers like Ransom out. The other responds that they did have a dog, Tartar, which they had used in an experiment. This is a minor detail, but one that illustrates well Lewis's method of caricature. As an antivivisectionist, Lewis enjoyed lampooning those willing to perform experiments on animals as people who might sacrifice a housepet, "man's best friend" even, in their relentless pursuit of information. Lewis had actually read of an experiment by some German scientists to keep a dog's head alive artificially.[1] He would find such an experiment utterly repulsive. Even the dog's name, Tartar, adds to the texture of the narrative. *Tartar* suggests Tartarus, the infernal regions of classical mythology. Throughout the Ransom trilogy, Lewis heaps all manner of diabolical or hellish imagery upon his villains, reminding his readers that their badness may be psychological or sociological, but it is also theological.

Besides Devine's flippancy and Weston's rudeness, this disreputable pair have all the earmarks of Lewisian scoundrels. Weston calls philology "unscientific foolery" (13) and dismisses history and the classics as trash (27). Having already disposed of the dog, Weston feels that in a properly governed country the simple-minded boy would be seized by the state for use in scientific experiments (14, 19). Devine, on his part, is interested in the "industrial side" of space travel (17). As for the inhabitants of Malacandra, Devine jokes that the brutes will all be exterminated, except for a few that Weston may sleep with or dissect or keep as pets (34). Despite his more courteous and well-mannered demeanor, Devine is judged by Ransom to be the more odious of his kidnappers because he is motivated by nothing but unblinking selfishness.

Weston's problem is that his abstract ideals about advancing his species are more real to him than actual beings or concrete ethical obligations. This becomes especially clear in the humorous scene when Weston's magniloquent speech to the Oyarsa is translated into Malacandrian by Ransom. Weston boasts about human civilization with its sophisticated commerce and transportation, among other things, and concludes that "our right to supersede you is the right of the higher over the lower" (135). Using concrete Malacandrian terms, Ransom comes up with this translation: "He says we exchange many things among ourselves and can carry heavy weights very quickly a long way. Because of all this, he says it would not be the act of a bent *hnau* if our people killed all your people" (136). A moment later when Weston begins a sentence with "She—," Ransom has to interrupt to ask who "She" is. "Life, of course," explains Weston irritably. For Weston "Life" is more real than actual living things. (Lewis noted in *The Discarded Image* [17] that "Life," a concrete term to biologists, had become a quasi-religious abstraction in the writings of Shaw, Wells, and Bergson.)

Apart from outright lies, the main way in which Lewis's evil characters abuse language is this kind of excessive abstraction. In *That Hideous Strength,* the irreplaceable Bragdon Wood becomes a pink area on a map. And Mark Studdock's sociological training produces a similar result: "His education had had the curious effect of making things that he read and wrote more real to him than things he saw. Statistics about agricultural labourers were the substance; any real ditcher, ploughman, or farmer's boy, was the shadow. Though he had never noticed it himself, he had a great reluctance, in his work, ever to use such words as 'man' or 'woman.' He preferred to write about 'vocational groups,' 'elements,' 'classes' and 'populations': for, in his own way, he believed as firmly as any mystic in the superior reality of the things that are not seen" (87).

Lewis's preference for concrete language is rooted in his Platonic ontology. Combining medieval ideas with those of his friend Owen Barfield, Lewis believed that God, the quintessence, is the most concrete being in the cosmos (see *RP* 87). Angels are less concrete than God but more concrete than humans and the physical world they inhabit. This can be seen in Augray's statement to Ransom that eldils are hard to see, not because they are nearly immaterial, but because our worlds are nearly immaterial to them. "To us," explains the sorn, "the *eldil* is a thin, half-real body that can go through walls and rocks: to himself he goes through them because he is solid and firm and they are like cloud" (*OSP* 95).

Those who move away from God continue to lose substance, to become less real. In *The Great Divorce,* for example, the lost souls who visit the outskirts of heaven are mere "man-shaped stains on the brightness of that air" whose steps do not even bend the blades of grass or disturb the dewdrops (27). Hell, the furthest place from God, represents almost total loss of substance. In *The Great Divorce* Lewis states that "the whole difficulty of understanding Hell is that the thing to be understood is so nearly Nothing" (75).

Of course, Lewis recognized the need for abstract language in analytic discourse, but he—like Orwell—lamented how often abstractions became euphemisms, turning reality into "nearly nothing." For him the use of concrete, definite language was a safeguard against replacing actualities with fanciful cognitive constructs. Part of the reason he valued poetry was that it represented "the skill of concrete utterance" (*PH* 114). He thought that all true lovers of poetry mouthed the words as they read, to get out the sounds of the words as well as their meaning (*LCSL* 152), and he claimed that all good poets loved proper names (*SIL* 115). Lewis's good characters are equally fond of poetry, while his bad characters dismiss it as "unscientific foolery." At St. Anne's in *That Hideous Strength,* the one who has no use for poetry is MacPhee, the humorless naysayer of the group (194).

Perelandra

In *Out of the Silent Planet* Weston and Devine are basically papier-mâché villains, characters whose badness is often comic. In *Perelandra* Lewis offers a more sinister and disturbing vision of evil. He also probes the origins of evil, showing how it could arise in a sympathetic character like Ransom or even in the unfallen Eve of another world.

One of the persistent questions of Christian theodicy is how evil could come into a universe created by a deity in whom there is no evil. The usual answer is that God created beings with a free will, allowing them the choice of good or evil. But then, one asks, if there was then no evil in the universe, where did the evil come from that the creatures might choose?

Lewis embraced the Augustinian view that evil is not the opposite of good but rather the absence of good—just as darkness is not really the opposite of light but rather the absence of light. (One can dispel darkness with just a point of light, a candle, but one cannot dispel light with a point of darkness.) In *Perelandra* Ransom learns that evil may come into a perfect world not because there are positive evils attempting to seduce him but because he is tempted to cling to good things desired over good things given.

This truth unfolds itself gradually in Ransom's mind. Not long after arriving on the planet, he tastes the nectar from a yellow fruit and finds it inexpressibly delicious: "It was like the discovery of a totally new *genus* of pleasures, something unheard of among men, out of all reckoning, beyond all covenant. For one draught of this on earth wars would be fought and nations betrayed" (42). Though both his palate and his reason tell him taste again, some obscurer instinct prevents him: "Perhaps the experience had been so complete that repetition would be a vulgarity—like asking to hear the same symphony twice in a day" (43).

The next day Ransom finds exquisite delight when he touches the bubble from a Perelandran bubble-tree and it bursts in his face. He feels the urge to plunge through the whole lot of bubbles to multiply the enchantment tenfold (48), but again he is restrained by some inner adviser. This time, though, he is able to identify the source of his restraint: "This itch to have things over again, as if life were a film that could be unrolled twice or even made to work backwards . . . was it possibly the root of all evil? No: of course the love of money was called that. But money itself—perhaps one valued it chiefly as a defence against chance, a security for being able to have things over again, a means of arresting the unrolling of the film" (48, ellipsis Lewis's). This lesson, learned from a fruit tree and a bubble-tree, becomes one of the predominant themes of *Perelandra.* Humans long for a godlike sovereignty over their lives, to maximize pleasure and security, to wall out pain and uncertainty. But only when they learn to accept vicissitudes and vulnerability as inherent to the fabric of life can they truly be free.

When Ransom later explains the nature of evil to the Green Lady, he amplifies this theme. Though she inhabits a world where everything is good, she herself could become the instrument by which evil enters in. Ransom reminds her that when she first saw him from afar, she thought he was her husband, from whom she had become separated. She had been disconcerted for a moment—only a moment—and then adjusted to the new circumstance. But, Ransom asks, what if she had clung to her old expectation, refusing to exchange her hope to find her husband for the novel experience of meeting someone from another world? (68) The Green Lady comprehends this, thinking of times she had gone looking for one kind of fruit and finding another: "One joy was expected and another is given. . . . You could send your soul after the good you had expected, instead of turning it to the good you had got. You could refuse the real good; you could make the real fruit taste insipid by thinking of the other" (69).

The Green Lady's recognition of how evil might enter into her heart applies at the cosmic level as well. Once he discovers that Weston has voyaged to Perelandra, Ransom feels he needs to explain about the evil—real, not hypothetical—that exists outside her world. Building on her understanding about taking the good that came instead of clinging to the old good, Ransom identifies the Bent One as an eldil who "clung longer—who has been clinging since before the worlds were made" (83). The Green Lady responds that the old good would cease to be good if one did that, and Ransom agrees: "Yes. It has ceased. And still he clings" (83). The Bent One (Lucifer) was granted one of the greatest of all goods—to be Maleldil's viceroy over a world. Yet he would accept no sovereign over him, considering equality with Maleldil as a thing to be grasped. And the temptation to which he fell becomes the one he will tempt humans with. Just as the serpent told Eve, "You shall be as gods," the Un-man tries to convince the Green Lady that, by disobeying Maleldil, she can take her place among eldils by imitating women of earth who became "little Maleldils" unto themselves (106). What the Un-man offers as a great glory, becoming a little Maleldil, is the same thing the sorns of Malacandra considered to be the root of the Earth's ills (*OSP* 102).

The principle of accepting what is given rather than clinging to what was expected is pictured throughout *Perelandra* in the image of riding with the wave rather than fighting the current. For example, when Ransom learns that his beloved hrossa and sorns of Malacandra will perish before other species because they live on a world more ancient than Earth or Perelandra, he is tempted to question the Grand Design. But the Green Lady explains to him: "They are their own part of the history and not another. We are on this side of the wave and they on the far side. All is new" (63). Later when Ransom tries to explain to her how humans would do anything to avoid dying, she replies: "But how can one wish any of those waves not to reach us which Maleldil is rolling towards us?" (68).

The image of riding the wave explains the thematic significance of the fixed land. Readers are often puzzled because the symbolism of the fixed land and the floating islands is the opposite of what they would have expected. Maleldil has decreed the floating islands to be the proper home of the king and queen of Perelandra, and he has forbidden them to dwell on the fixed land. At first thought, one would tend to associate a fixed land with absolutes, eternal truths, anchoring oneself in unchanging realities. And floating islands would connote the opposite—relativism, instability, being driven by the caprices of the moment. In the Epistle of James the doubter is described as being "like a wave of the sea driven with the wind and tossed" (1:6, KJV). And in Spenser the wandering islands are to be avoided by the righteous.

But for Lewis the emphasis is not upon stability vs. instability but upon relinquishing control and accepting what is given. When Ransom wonders if Maleldil had told the king how the queen's temptation would turn out, the king answers, "He gave me no assurance. No fixed land. Always one must throw oneself into the wave" (210).

This imagery that recurs throughout *Perelandra* gains added poignancy when we find it again in *Surprised by Joy:* "With my mother's death all settled happiness, all that was tranquil and reliable, disappeared from my life. There was to be much fun, many pleasures, many stabs of Joy; but no more of the old security. It was sea and islands now; the great continent had sunk like Atlantis" (21).

One rather suspects that Lewis's doctrine of learning to be carried on the wave rather than craving the fixed land may have been derived in part from his learning to accept the untimely loss of his mother.

Evil does not come to Perelandra from either Ransom or the Green Lady clinging too long to the good desired rather than the good that is given. Rather, evil arrives from outside, from the fallen planet, in the person of Weston. As Ransom discovers within himself the origins of evil, Weston illustrates the final destiny of those who succumb to evil. When Weston tries to ally himself to spiritual forces he does not really understand, he loses his selfhood: the man becomes Un-man.

Though the Un-man seems like the devil incarnate, there are times when Ransom is not sure if something of Weston still resides in that walking carcass. In one of the moments in which the pitiful Weston-voice breaks through, it complains, "I'm down in the bottom of a big black hole" (129). This cryptic image is repeated but never really elaborated, so readers may come away from *Perelandra* without a very clear sense of its significance for Lewis.

Examining the image of the black hole in Lewis's other works, however, reveals more fully its implications in *Perelandra.* In *The Last Battle,* for example, the dwarves—those who pride themselves on not being "taken in"—enter the stable with Tirian and the others. But where the others find a new, unspoiled and unspoilable Narnia, the dwarves see nothing but a smelly stable and complain of the black hole they are in, clearly one of their own making. Similarly, in *The Pilgrim's Regress,* the protagonist, John, worries that the Landlord (God) will put him in a "black hole full of snakes" because John has not been keeping the rules well enough (23). John becomes so obsessed with an angry Landlord putting people in a black hole (27–28) that he is elated when he comes to believe that there really is no Landlord and no black hole (38). In the end, though, John learns from his guide that there is a Landlord, but not one who invented a black hole just for punishment: "The Landlord does not make the blackness. The blackness is there already. . . . What do you mean by a hole? Something that ends. A black hole is blackness enclosed, limited. And in that sense the Landlord *has* made the black hole. He has put into the world a Worst Thing. . . . It is the Landlord's last service to those who will let him do nothing better for them" (181). Weston's black hole is likewise an abyss of his own making, the culmination of his own decisions and inclinations. Weston may say with Milton's Satan, "Myself am hell."

That Hideous Strength

Ransom's encounters with evil in the first two books of the trilogy provide the context for understanding the people at N.I.C.E. in *That Hideous Strength.* N.I.C.E. represents the values of Weston and Devine writ large. Weston is revered at N.I.C.E. as a great scientist murdered on one of his interplanetary travels, and Devine reappears as Lord Feverstone (a rather infernal title). The dreamer and the schemer have spawned at N.I.C.E. a whole academy of dreamers and schemers.

In his homily "The Inner Ring," Lewis speaks about people who become scoundrels by degrees, making increasingly serious compromises of their integrity and values in order to make their way into an exclusive circle, then the circle-within-the-circle. Mark Studdock is quite clearly a victim of the inner-ring syndrome as he tries to gain acceptance at N.I.C.E. He is willing to put up with pompous bureaucrats like Busby and Curry just for the pleasure of being an insider in the Progressive Element. Then he is liberated to see Feverstone baiting these two boors and inviting him to join a more elite set of insiders. As he gets more enmeshed in the machinations at N.I.C.E., Mark finds it harder and harder to tell who really is on the inside and who is just a "mascot." Even Filostrato, who dismisses most everyone else at Belbury as *canaglia* (plebians), is not a true insider; he knows about the living head at N.I.C.E., but he does not know—until too late—that it is not his science that keeps the head alive. In "The Inner Ring" Lewis warns that trying to penetrate all the inner circles is like peeling an onion (*WG* 64). In the center there is nothing.

Mark's attempted ascent up the organizational ladder is actually a descent into hell. The many references to the inner rings, inner circles, and wheels-within-wheels make plain Mark's inner-ring syndrome. However, these allusions also reveal a less obvious subtext: Mark's experiences at N.I.C.E. closely parallel Dante's trek through the Inferno.

The Divine Comedy was never very far from Lewis's mind. He first read the poem, in Dante's medieval Italian, during his midteens while studying with Kirkpatrick. He read and reread Dante's masterwork for the rest of his life, often praising it in his letters. According to George Sayer, Lewis considered Dante the most sublime of all poets and judged the "Paradiso" to be the greatest poetic achievement in European literature.[2] Lewis used the "Paradiso" as his structural subtext in *The Great Divorce;* in *That Hideous Strength,* published in the same year, he used the "Inferno" as his structural subtext.

Like the discourse of Weston and Devine in *Out of the Silent Planet,* the conversation of the people at N.I.C.E. is peppered with hellish rhetoric. In the sections of *That Hideous Strength* devoted to Bracton and Belbury, there are nearly eighty phrases such as "raise hell," "the devil of a stink," "I'm damned," "these infernal college politics," "what in the blazes," and so forth. These sections also contain more specific Dantean echoes. In describing Wither, the deputy director of N.I.C.E., as one of those "souls who have lost the intellectual good" (213), Lewis is translating from "The Inferno": "c'hanno perduto il ben dell'intelletto" (3, 18). Later when Wither impassively looks upon his own death and perdition (353), the narrator comments, "So full of sleep are they at the time when they leave the right way," taken directly from canto 1, lines 11–12.

In general, there is a close correlation between Mark's increasing entanglement in the affairs of N.I.C.E. and Dante's journey through the circles of hell, guided by the poet Virgil. The narrator of "The Inferno" (designated here as Dante, for convenience) begins his passage at the vestibule of hell, where he sees the opportunists, those who served neither good nor evil, but only themselves. The first person from Bracton College who appears in *That Hideous Strength* is Curry, the officious subwarden. Feverstone describes

Curry as "a man who loves business and wire-pulling for their own sake and doesn't really ask what it's all about" (40). Curry is not necessarily evil; he is just someone who thrives on college politics. Accordingly, when the great conflagration comes to Belbury at the end of the story, Curry is the only one associated with N.I.C.E. who survives.

The first circle of the inferno is Limbo, the abode of virtuous pagans. There Dante meets the great poets and philosophers who lived before the time of Christ and so could not benefit from his atoning work. Curry mentions to Mark early on that there will be resistance to the plans of N.I.C.E. from the likes of Hingest (a true research scientist), Glossop (a classics scholar), and Jewel (the college canon). These men are not directly allied with Ransom and the followers of Maleldil, but neither will they be any part of N.I.C.E. When Jewel tries to argue at the faculty meeting against the sale of Bragdon Wood, he is so feeble and so upset that his voice is barely audible, and Feverstone mocks him into silence (28). This may allude to the virtuous pagans in circle one who speak with muted voices (4, 114).

In the second circle, Dante encounters those who sinned through carnal desire. In the next section of *That Hideous Strength,* after the one in which Jewel is humiliated, Jane is asked by Mrs. Dimble about her sex life and then bursts into tears (30). We have already learned from the opening pages of the novel that Mark pays little attention to Jane; when he comes to bed, he has little to say to her, and only one thing can keep him awake—and that not for long (14). Later, when Mark gradually comes to see the emptiness and squalor of his life, he feels that somehow he has violated his wife, made her the object of his lust, not his companion in love (247, 381). It would seem that Mark himself best exemplifies the carnal sinner.

In the third circle are the gluttons, those who overindulge in food and drink. In the next section of *That Hideous Strength,* Mark has dinner with Feverstone and Busby in the Curry's rooms. Busby is described as "busily engaged in eating" during the conversation, and he has to wipe his beard before speaking up (36). Busby is also described as having a third glass of wine, which loosens his tongue and makes him easy prey for the glib Feverstone (37). Mark also enjoys the excellent port being served, and he is "not perfectly sober" when he returns home to Jane that evening (46). Throughout the rest of the story, Lewis emphasizes all the heavy drinking that goes on at N.I.C.E., including Mark's increased reliance on alcohol.

In the fourth circle, Dante witnesses a battle between the avaricious and the prodigals, those who cling too much to material things and those who waste material things. The same kind of conflict arises when Feverstone, the spendthrift, mocks the aspirations of Busby and Curry. Busby, enraptured by the program of N.I.C.E., exclaims upon "the buildings alone, the apparatus alone! . . . Fifteen department directors at fifteen thousand a year each!" (37) When Feverstone offers a mocking reply about "careers for our sons," Curry takes Busby's side and rhapsodizes about the Pragmatometer, a device to coordinate all the research activities that will cost half a million (38). Feverstone dismisses all this to Mark as drivel. He is the same Dick Devine he was in *Out of the Silent Planet;* his only real concern is how he personally can benefit from all this. And we assume he is benefiting when we see him in the next scene driving recklessly in a flashy, big car, taking Mark to N.I.C.E.

In the fifth circle of hell are the wrathful and the sullen. And when Mark arrives at Belbury, he is assigned to work with Steele and Cosser, who are both wrathful and sullen. Steele is "a tall, unsmiling man," who complains that Mark has been unloaded on his department without anyone consulting him (58–59). At their first meeting, Cosser and Steele talk about Mark as if he is not even there, but later Cosser confides to Mark, while picking his nose, that he hopes to get rid of Steele and take over his position (85–86).

As he continues at N.I.C.E., Mark encounters more and more sinister colleagues. The repulsively obese Professor Filostrato, the sadistic Fairy Hardcastle, and "Mad Parson" Straik make self-important functionaries like Curry and Busby seem almost likable. Straik's rambling diatribes are loaded with biblical phrases and motifs, but his ideas sound like those of an anti-Christ. He ludicrously misapplies verse after verse from Scripture to advocate violence, coercive collectivism, and extermination of any who resist (78–80). He certainly parallels those whom Dante finds in the sixth circle of hell—the heretics.

This pattern continues until the final judgment of everyone at N.I.C.E. In the seventh circle of the inferno are the violent, those who do violence to nature and violence to others. And succeeding pages in *That Hideous Strength* describe what sounds like a murder outside the Common Room of Bracton (93), Fairy Hardcastle's arousal when inflicting pain (96), and the noise of animals being tortured in the name of science (102).

In the eighth circle are the fraudulent. And in the next section of the novel, Mark discovers that his position at Bracton has been fraudulently taken away from him (105–6), and Feverstone fraudulently denies any responsibility (111). Mark himself joins in the fraud, writing newspaper editorials that blame Jews, lawyers, and other resisting elements for riots that were engineered by the secret police at N.I.C.E. (131–34).

The ninth circle of hell is reserved for the worst of offenders, those who betray kindred, country, and their faith. Mark has been carnal, gluttonous, greedy, prodigal, and fraudulent. But he stops short of the most serious crimes he might commit in the service of N.I.C.E. The whole reason that Mark was recruited in the first place was not for his work as a sociologist but so that Frost and Wither could get their hands on his wife, to make use of her power of second sight. Not realizing its significance at first, Mark balks at the whole idea of bringing Jane to Belbury: "Her mere presence would have made all the laughter of the Inner Ring sound metallic, unreal; and what he now regarded as common prudence would seem to her, and through her to himself, mere flattery, back-biting and toad-eating" (171). As Wither and the others put increasing pressure on Mark to turn her over to them, his resistance too increases: "For almost the first time in his life a gleam of something like disinterested love came into his mind; he wished he had never married her, never dragged her into this whole outfit of horrors which was, apparently, to be his life" (185–86). Besides his refusal to betray his wife, Mark also refuses to trample on a cross, as discussed in chapter 2. It would seem that in the last circle of his own descent, he finally discovers the moral core within himself, which will allow for his escape.

The sinners in "The Inferno" are already suffering, but the sinners at N.I.C.E. will receive their punishment all at once. In the closing chapters of *That Hideous Strength* especially, images from the final cantos of "The Inferno" predominate. When Frost and Wither, the leaders of N.I.C.E. and the two most depraved characters in the story, lock into a bizarre embrace and fall onto the floor, seeming to wrestle without moving (243), they recall the two brothers in "The Inferno" who had quarreled all their lives and are frozen together for eternity in a sheet of ice (32, 40–60). When Filostrato and Straik are both decapitated as a sacrifice to the dark eldils (354–55), their fate echoes the beheadings and dismemberments of the schismatics and heretics in the ninth circle (canto 38).

Mark, who found his moral bearings just in time, is spared from the carnage at the end of *That Hideous Strength.* Yet his part in the story is also related with Dantean images and phrasing. When Mark sees an elephant join in with the other animals venting their rage on their tormentors at the banquet, the elephant is described as standing with "its ears standing stiffly out like the devil's wings on each side of its head" (349). This image comes directly from "The Inferno"; at the very center of hell sits Satan, frozen in ice, with batlike wings fluttering at the sides of his head (34, 38–54). As he watches the elephant carelessly trampling people and glorying in the destruction, Mark calls him "the King of the world" (350); this phrase seems less odd when one compares it to Dante's description of Satan as "the emperor of his sad world" (34, 28). Mark loses consciousness briefly, but he is told by Merlin to "get up," to make good his escape (352). The words "Get up" are used to translate Virgil's words—*Levati su*—when he stirs Dante to shake off his stupor and escape the lowest circle of the inferno (34, 94).

One of the most unforgettably grotesque images in "The Inferno" is that of Lucifer gnawing on the skulls of Brutus and Cassius, betrayers of Caesar, and Judas, betrayer of Christ. The idea that Satan devours the condemned is taken literally—and whimsically—by Lewis in "Screwtape Proposes a Toast," where Screwtape is the after-dinner speaker at a banquet of devils feasting on human souls. Used more obliquely in the trilogy, the Dantean image suggests two more traits shared by Lewis's evil characters: abuse of intellect and self-destruction.

Dante's phrase rendered by Lewis as "souls who lose the intellectual good" may be interpreted to mean those who lose the good of intellect or those who do not use intellect for good. Weston and Devine are pronounced only half hnau on Malacandra because they have their rational faculties but no moral sense. Their science is not tempered by conscience. In the same way, the major figures at N.I.C.E. all abuse their intellects and deny their moral instincts. Wither habitually uses evasive, circumlocutory speech to disguise his true aims and to manipulate others. Frost convinces himself that all moral responses are mere by-products of biochemical processes. Straik takes biblical phrases wildly out of context in order to make them seem to support his violent radicalism and blasphemous deification of humans.

All of these who habitually abuse language have their powers of speech taken from them. The epigraph of *That Hideous Strength* explains that the title of the book is taken from a poem by Sir David Lyndsay describing the tower of Babel. N.I.C.E. is a new Babel, another attempt to marshal human resources to clamber up to heaven, or to bring heaven to earth by main force. In the end, these new Nimrods experience another confusion of tongues and achieve only their own destruction.

Like Weston in *Perelandra,* the leaders of N.I.C.E. are destroyed by the forces that they themselves have set into motion. Weston called a force into himself that did indeed come in and take over. Filostrato and Straik would sacrifice human lives so that they may rule as gods, but they end up themselves as human sacrifices. Feverstone, who hopes to subdue the earth, is swallowed up by the earth. Frost, who denies the reality of the passions, is consumed in flames that he ignites himself. The others, who have been destroying animals for trivial causes, are destroyed by liberated animals. In the end, the banquet at Belbury is another devils' banquet.

5

Ransom and Lewis: Cosmic Voyage as Spiritual Pilgrimage

> *Perhaps in the eyes of the gods the true use of a book lies in its effects upon the author. You remember what Ibsen said, that every play he wrote had been written for the purgation of his own heart.*
>
> C. S. Lewis, letter to A. Greeves, 28 August 1930

A SEMINAL MOMENT for both the Ransom trilogy and for the *Lord of the Rings* epic was the day Lewis declared to Tolkien that the sort of stories they both delighted in was not being written anymore, so that the two of them should begin creating such stories for themselves.[1] Indeed, Lewis must have enjoyed writing the trilogy as much as he had earlier enjoyed reading the fantasies of Macdonald, Morris, and Chesterton. For the Ransom stories gave Lewis the opportunity to re-present Christian doctrines in a new imaginative context, to recover the awe and majesty of the medieval world-picture, and to offer his own reflections on the nature of good and evil. But beyond these conscious purposes, the writing of these fantasies seemed to feed some obscurer hunger in Lewis as well.

Biographer A. N. Wilson has aptly noted that Lewis wrote the *Chronicles of Narnia* "for the child who was within himself."[2] Indeed, the "uniquely persisting child's sense of wonder and nightmare" noticed by those who knew Lewis is evident on every page of the chronicles. The Ransom trilogy, though less overtly, reveals as well an author grappling with the child inside him and retracing some of the key steps in his own spiritual pilgrimage.

Lewis explained on several occasions that his method for writing what he called "theologised science fiction" came from David Lindsay's *Voyage to Arcturus.* Lewis was not at all attracted to the theme of *Voyage to Arcturus,* but he was fascinated by its method. He saw in Lindsay new possibilities for using the popular genres of science fiction and fantasy to explore psychological and spiritual themes. Lewis wrote about Lindsay's novel: "His Tormance [the fictional planet of *Voyage*] is a region of the spirit. He is the first writer to discover what 'other planets' are really good for in fiction. No merely physical strangeness or merely spatial distance will realize the idea of otherness which is what we are always trying to grasp in a story about voyaging through space: you must go into another dimension. To construct plausible and moving 'other worlds' you must draw on the only real 'other world' we know, that of the spirit" (*OOW* 12). This is an apt description of Lewis's own narrative strategy in his fantasy writing. The creatures and events one encounters in the Ransom trilogy certainly point to the unseen realities Lewis believed in, but they also reveal, perhaps more than he realized, the contours of his own consciousness, the "other world" of his own spirit.

Out of the Silent Planet

In the first paragraph of *Out of the Silent Planet,* the protagonist is not introduced by name but rather referred to as "the Pedestrian" (7). The term seems appropriate enough to describe a man on a walking tour, waiting out a thundershower under a chestnut tree. But the word is capitalized all three times, as if referring to a character out of Bunyan, one whose outer journeys will reflect his soul's progress.

The word *pedestrian* also suggests that which is ordinary, uneventful, even humdrum. The last thing the Pedestrian in the story wants is an adventure (11); but he is about to be drawn, willy-nilly, into adventure on a cosmic scale. Lewis, like Tolkien, reveled in stories where ordinary people are asked to enact extraordinary deeds—where a kingdom is saved by a fishmonger's son, or where the fate of a world rests upon the faithfulness of a hobbit. For both writers such stories reflected their belief, as Christians, that ordinary mortals have immortal souls, and anyone may be called upon to engage in spiritual warfare with unseen powers.

In the second paragraph the Pedestrian is identified as Ransom, a Cambridge philologist on a solitary walking tour. He is a tall, round-shouldered man, thirty-five to forty, with "that particular kind of shabbiness which marks a member of the intelligentsia on a holiday" (7). At first glance, one cannot help but notice how much this description resembles Lewis himself. He was in his late thirties when he wrote *Out of the Silent Planet.* He was of middle height, and he has been described as round-shouldered by more than one who knew him.[3] And his shabbiness as a dresser was legendary. Those who first met him often thought he looked more like a gardener, a butcher, or a country farmer than a university don.[4]

Lewis was at Oxford when he wrote *Out of the Silent Planet,* not Cambridge. And his specialty was literature, not language—though he could certainly qualify as a philologist, given his knowledge of classical Greek and Latin; Anglo-Saxon; medieval English, French, Latin, and Icelandic; and modern French, German, and Italian.

Continuing in *Out of the Silent Planet,* readers soon learn that Ransom is a bachelor (17), an antivivisectionist (27), a Christian (35), and one who considers himself handy in the kitchen (37). All of these traits remind us again of the author himself. Lewis commented that Ransom was not meant to be a self-portrait.[5] But whatever his intentions, he created in Ransom a character whose convictions and consciousness largely resemble his own.

The opening pages of *Out of the Silent Planet* describe experiences that Lewis might have had on any one of his walking tours. Once Ransom stumbles upon Weston and Devine, however, his adventures soon begin in earnest. Sensing something vaguely criminal about their intentions toward a simpleminded boy who works for them, Ransom nevertheless accepts a drink from Devine, discovering too late that it has been drugged. He loses consciousness and experiences a nightmare that has left many readers puzzled.

This dream marks Ransom's departure from the world of the

ordinary and his entry into Other Worlds. In his drug-induced sleep, Ransom dreams that he, Devine, and Weston are in a sunlit, walled garden surrounded by darkness (18). Weston and Devine climb over the wall, and Ransom follows them far enough to straddle it, sitting on his coat to protect himself from the broken bottles. (In Britain and elsewhere in Europe, stone walls may have broken bottles embedded in the mortar on top to discourage anyone from trying to climb over.) Before Ransom can get over, however, a door opens in the wall from the outside and some creatures bring back Devine and Weston, locking them in. Ransom is left straddling the wall, half in, half out of the garden.

This dream makes little sense to one reading *Out of the Silent Planet* for the first time, but further readings show it to be a symbolic adumbration of Ransom's adventures on Malacandra and on Perelandra. The garden represents planet earth. Weston and Devine will indeed try to escape the confines of this garden, taking Ransom with them. They will be forcibly returned to earth by creatures not of this planet. And the whole adventure will leave Ransom with a dual identity—partly a dweller of this world, partly one called to errands on other worlds. The motif of Ransom's dual identity will emerge even more clearly in *Perelandra.* Ransom's dream-passage into the Other World is also a synopsis of his pilgrimage that is just beginning.

When he starts to come to, Ransom makes a feeble attempt to escape, but he is soon knocked unconscious again. Awakening the next time in an eerie metallic chamber, he thinks at first that he "might be dead and already in the ghost-life" (22) and then feels he is "poised on a sort of emotional watershed from which, he felt, he might at any moment pass into delirious terror or into an ecstasy of joy" (23). Lewis associates the ecstasy and dread of this moment with a dazzling, oppressive radiance coming in from the skylight. At first he thinks it is just the moon, though "he had never seen such a moon—so white, so blinding and so large" (21–22). This moon is preternaturally large and seems to be getting larger every moment, a "megalomaniac disk" (23). When Weston enters and explains matter-of-factly that the orb they see is the planet earth, Ransom's response is revealingly phrased: " 'You mean we're—in space?' Ransom uttered the word with difficulty as a frightened child speaks of ghosts or a frightened man of cancer" (25).

The images used here to evoke Ransom's terror—the oppressively brilliant moon, the mention of ghosts and of cancer—all harken back to Lewis's own childhood fears and traumas as described in *Surprised by Joy.* Some of the most powerfully written passages in the trilogy are those in which the "frightened child" whom Lewis remembered only too well, whom he carried inside him, found expression. As Lewis explained in one of his letters to children, "You see, I don't think age matters so much as people think. Parts of me are still 12 and I think other parts were already 50 when I was 12" (*LTC* 34).

Overcoming fears is one of the recurring preoccupations of the trilogy, especially in *Out of the Silent Planet.* Though Ransom is a Cambridge don, a distinguished linguist, and a pious man, his attainments and beliefs are not a very present help in time of trouble. In fact, Chad Walsh has correctly noted that Ransom's "one besetting sin is anxiety."[6] Lewis called the first book of the trilogy "Ransom's *enfance,*"[7] portraying Ransom as a man who, though in his middle years, is in his soul's childhood.

On the voyage to Malacandra, Ransom indeed has excellent reasons to be afraid. He has been drugged, knocked over the head, kidnapped, dragged into outer space, and he has overheard a conversation about his being turned over to some alien beings called sorns. This last bit of news plays havoc with his already overcharged imagination.

> His mind, like so many minds of his generation, was richly furnished with bogies. He had read his H. G. Wells and others. His universe was peopled with horrors such as ancient and medieval mythology could hardly rival. No insect-like, vermiculate or crustacean Abominable, no twitching feelers, rasping wings, slimy coils, curling tentacles, no monstrous union of superhuman intelligence and insatiable cruelty seemed to him anything but likely on an alien world. . . . He saw in imagination various incompatible monstrosities—bulbous eyes, grinning jaws, horns, stings, mandibles. Loathing of insects, loathing of snakes, loathing of things that

> squashed and squelched, all played their horrible symphonies over his nerves. (35)

Lewis's horrific imagery here recalls the other childhood fear of insects, which receives prominent attention in *Surprised by Joy* (8–9). This passage is significant as well because it presents a character in a fantasy story whose imagination has been adversely conditioned by the fantasy stories he has read. This is an early clue of Lewis's intention to engage in some counterconditioning of his own sort.

But with childhood nightmares comes the child's sense of wonder. After an unpleasant descent to Malacandra (discussed in chapter 3), Ransom's first sight of the Malacandrian terrain fills him with unexpected pleasure. He sees "a pale blue sky—a fine winter-morning sky it would have been on Earth—a great billowy cumular mass of rose-colour lower down which he took for a cloud" (41). After learning to interpret all his novel perceptions, Ransom finds perspective: "His first impression was of a bright, pale world—a water-colour world out of a child's paint-box; a moment later he recognized the flat belt of light blue as a sheet of water, or of something like water, which came nearly to his feet" (42).

Readers not acquainted with Lewis might read this as relatively neutral description of an alien terrain. But those who have read a Lewis biography or his letters should recognize that his imagination would revel in virtually every detail he mentions here. The image of a child's paint-box would surely rekindle memories of little Jack and Warnie at home in Ireland before their mother's death, creating elaborate worlds and illustrating their creations with charming and surprisingly sure-handed watercolors. The "fine winter sky" of Malacandra and "pale blue" waters were both favorites of his, mentioned in letters of his in which he delights in the beauty of nature. (See, for example, *TST* 338, 373, 406.)[8] Even Lewis's conception of those towering, rose-tinted cloudlike cliffs of Malacandra may owe something to a particularly evocative, almost epiphanic, experience of nature that Lewis had described in detail to Arthur Greeves a few years before.

> My second delightful moment was of a different kind, and takes a little arrangement to describe. Imagine first a pure rosy pink sunset: in the extreme distance a sky covered with thin "mackerel" as delicate as the veins in a shell, & all pink: in the foreground, blackly outlined against this, huge crags and castles and Valkyrie-shapes of cloud. Got that? Now;—imagine that all this existed only for a fraction of [a] second, the pink light being in fact no sunset but a vast flood of summer lightening [*sic*]: so that all those beetling cliffs and tottering cities of the gods, together with the rosy flush behind which made them visible, had leaped out of pure star-set darkness an instant before, and vanished into it instantaneously again—and so times without number. (*TST* 389)

Whether or not Lewis had this particular experience in mind when he created the Malacandrian landscape, it is clear that the environment of this world is congenial to his imagination.

Lewis's use of imagery in *Out of the Silent Planet* might be questioned at this point. His negative references to ghosts, insects, snakes, and the like are universally understood, whereas the imaginative pleasure he took in writing about the Malacandrian landscape may not be fully recognized by his readers. In any case, Lewis does make it clear what Ransom's response is: "Before anything else he learned that Malacandra was beautiful" (42).

Despite the beauty of the landscape, Ransom still has those dreaded sorns to contend with. Once he has seen the sorns, Ransom again dwells upon childhood fears: "They were quite unlike the horrors his imagination had conjured up, and for that reason had taken him off his guard. They appealed away from the Wellsian fantasies to an earlier, almost an infantile, complex of fears. Giants—ogres—ghosts—skeletons: those were its key words" (47). Even after Ransom has spent months among the hrossa, the gentle otterlike poets of Malacandra whom he has come to love and trust, his old fears reemerge once he begins his journey to the cave of the sorn Augray (86, 88).

But like most everything else on Malacandra, Augray is a pleasant surprise to Ransom. Though he looks like a "goblin" or a "gawk" and moves with "strange spidery movements" (92, 93), Augray reveals sorns to be the thinkers and shepherds of the planet, different certainly from the hrossa, but no less beneficent. The rapidity with which Ransom overcomes his initial apprehensions about Augray and the other sorns suggests that his time spent in this quirky sort of paradise has begun the process of healing his childhood complex of fears.

This process of healing is even more apparent when Ransom meets a member of another species on the planet, a pfifltrigg.

> Ransom . . . was glad that he had not met one of this third race on his first arrival in Malacandra. It was much more insect-like or reptilian than anything he had yet seen. . . . The insect-like effect was due to the speed and jerkiness of its movements and to the fact that it could swivel its head almost all the way round like a mantis; and it was increased by a kind of dry, rasping, jingling quality in the noise of its moving. It was rather like a grasshopper, rather like one of Arthur Rackham's dwarfs, rather like a frog, and rather like a little, old taxidermist whom Ransom knew in London. (112–13)

At first sight, this pfifltrigg would seem to qualify as one of those Wellsian abominables that haunt Ransom's imagination. But in this description, the horrific is replaced by the comic. In fact, Ransom has to stifle a laugh soon afterward, as he watches this creature, of the race of Malacandra's craftsmen and artisans, going to work on Ransom's portrait. The allusion to Rackham, one of Lewis's favorite illustrators and the one who evoked "Northernness" in him, further adds a benign tone to an encounter we might have expected to induce fear and loathing.

For Malacandra is a benign otherworld of the imagination, an unfallen planet where childhood wonders may literally exist and where childhood fears may be banished. Just as Augray helps Ransom overcome his nursery-room fears of ghosts and goblins, these pfifltriggi help him overcome his nursery-room fear of insects. And one supposes they may also have had therapeutic effects for the author.

The great trauma of Lewis's childhood, the death of his mother when he was nine, seems to be addressed in this benign otherworld as well. As recounted in chapter 1, the young Lewis's grief was intensified by the terror he felt when having to view his mother's corpse and by the horror he felt at the funeral service. In the Malacandrian funeral ritual for the three hrossa killed by Weston and Devine, one senses again the author drawing upon the healing powers of imagination. As the diverse creatures of the planet begin a funeral hymn, Ransom is gradually able to grasp its meaning: "Through his knowledge of the creatures and his love for them he began, ever so little, to hear it with their ears. A sense of great masses moving at visionary speeds, of giants dancing, of eternal sorrows eternally consoled, of he knew not what and yet what he had always known, awoke in him with the very first bars of the deep-mouthed dirge, and bowed down his spirit as if the gate of heaven had opened before him" (131).

"Let it go hence," the Malacandrian dirge begins; "Let it go hence, dissolve and be no body" (131). These opening words are especially poignant when one reads the account by Warren Lewis of the death of his and Jack's mother: "She died on my father's birthday, the 23rd of August: there was a Shakespearean calendar hanging on the wall of the room where she died, and my father preserved for the rest of his life the leaf for that day, with its quotation: 'Men must endure their *going hence*' " (*LCSL* 3).

After the funeral song, one of the attendants places something crystal near each body, and they disappear in a blinding flash, their spirits journeying upward with nothing remaining behind. Devine, with his usual crudity, makes an ill-timed quip about solving the murderer's problem of the body (132); yet one senses that such a spectacular exit also solves "the problem of the body" that so terrified the young Lewis at his mother's funeral.

Before returning to his home planet, which will never again quite be his home, Ransom receives this farewell counsel from the presiding spirit of Malacandra: "You are guilty of no evil, Ransom of Thulcandra, except a little fearfulness. For that, the journey you go on is your pain, and perhaps your cure: for you must be either mad or brave before it is ended" (142). The return flight is indeed a difficult one, and Ransom does indeed emerge largely cleansed of his fears. But a great deal of this cure has already taken place on Malacandra itself. One can see how different a person Ransom has become by comparing his terror at watching the "Earthrise" from space early in the story (22–24) to his exultant memories of watching the planet Jupiter rise from Malacandra in the closing pages of the book (159–60). In a similar manner, Lewis makes recurring references in *Surprised by Joy* to those ghastly full-moon nights he endured at the first boarding school he attended after his mother's death. Yet his letters and stories written as an adult reveal a consistent pleasure in the dazzling majesty of a full moon on a clear night. (Note also in *That Hideous Strength* how a brilliant full moon strikes fear into Mark Studdock the night he is introduced to the head [175–77], but Jane Studdock, secure at St. Anne's, finds the same moon exhilarating [194].)

Perelandra

The second book of the trilogy takes up the theme of learning to overcome fearfulness. This time, however, the apprehensions are not those of Ransom but of "Lewis," the author presenting himself as a character in the novel. Since Lewis is the one who had written up Ransom's adventures on Malacandra, he is fairly certain when he receives an urgent summons from Ransom that it has something to do with "inter-planetary politics" (10).

The character of "Lewis" at the beginning of *Perelandra* reminds us a great deal of Ransom at the beginning of *Out of the Silent Planet.* He finds himself walking alone with growing uneasiness as night falls. Just as "the last thing Ransom wanted was an adventure" (*OSP* 11), the last thing "Lewis" wants is to be "drawn in." He has no desire to encounter one of these unearthly creatures Ransom has been consorting with or to find himself suddenly beyond the point of no return: "I suppose every one knows this fear of getting 'drawn in'—the moment at which a man realises that what seemed mere speculations are on the point of landing him in the Communist Party or the Christian Church—the sense that a door has just slammed and left him on the inside" (*Per* 10).

As one might expect, "Lewis" the narrator is speaking here with an undisguised voice for Lewis the author. In *Surprised by Joy* Lewis describes his own conversion to Christianity in just the same terms, including even the image of the door. On the verge of accepting the claims of Christianity, Lewis reports that he felt a full sense of free will: "I could open the door or keep it shut" (*SBJ* 224). Once inside, though, he recognized that conversion meant not just intellectual assent, but it demanded surrender to another Will, a relinquishing of his lifelong desire "not to be interfered with."

As he approaches Ransom's remote cottage, "Lewis's" insecurity is intensified when he discovers that he has left his rucksack aboard the train, now miles away. Again, this detail reminds us of Ransom, who had originally been "drawn in," had committed himself inadvertently to his adventure, when he tossed his pack over the tall hedge at what turned out to be Weston's laboratory (*OSP* 10). As he made one desperate attempt to escape the clutches of Weston and Devine after they had drugged him, Ransom rushed to the exit: "For one glorious moment the door was open, the fresh night air was in his face, he saw the reassuring stars and even his own pack lying in the porch." But then he is struck over the head, and he feels "strong hands pulling him back into the dark passage, and the sound of a closing door" (*OSP* 20). Since Lewis himself always carried such a rucksack on his own walking tours and surely misplaced it a time or two,[9] losing one's pack at the beginning of a journey would make a natural image of having to relinquish one's earthly securities before commencing a spiritual journey. Again, in the image of setting aside the pack, Lewis's pilgrim reminds us of Bunyan's.

The fears of "Lewis" as he approaches Ransom's cottage are even more intense—and less justified—than those of Ransom in *Out of the Silent Planet.* Even though there is no visible danger or villainy to confront, "Lewis" fears he is on the edge of madness and actually has to bite his lip to keep from screaming (*Per* 13–14). He finally reaches the cottage and then pauses, trying to decide what to do: "At least I could try the door to see if it were really unlocked. I did. And it was. Next moment, I hardly know how, I found myself inside and let it slam behind me" (16). How fraught with suggestiveness are these deceptively simple sentences!

Once Ransom returns and tries to reassure "Lewis," there is a dramatic contrast between Ransom and "Lewis" in their interaction with the otherworldly. Ransom's serenity in the face of the supernatural, his matter-of-fact bravery about venturing off naked and alone to a new planet, contrasts starkly with the "Lewis," who resembles more the fear-ridden Ransom being carried to Malacandra in *Out of the Silent Planet.* The opening pages of *Perelandra* show that Ransom has traveled far in his spiritual pilgrimage; but succeeding pages will show that he has far yet to go. If the great challenge of his first journey was to overcome his fears, the great challenge of his second journey will be to overcome his doubts.

While Ransom found Malacandra to be surprisingly beautiful when he first arrived there, he is positively ravished with pleasure upon plummeting into the ocean of Perelandra. With warm subtropical seas surrounding him and the golden dome of a sky above him ("like the background of a medieval picture" [35]), Ransom finds that even an accidental mouthful of water from a passing wave gives him "quite astonishing pleasure . . . almost like meeting Pleasure itself for the first time" (35). Even the violent squall that rises up leaves him more dazzled than frightened. The thunder is more resonant than terrestrial thunder, making a kind of tinkling sound in the distance, "the laugh, rather than the roar, of heaven" (37). The repeated flashes of lightning on the multicolored water make him feel that he is at the center of a rainbow (38).

One reader complained to Lewis that the description of Perelandra made him seasick; another thought that surely this must be the stuff of nightmares.[10] But Ransom's rapture in the new world reflects again the author's own pleasures. Lewis described himself in *Surprised by Joy* as "passionately fond of water" (174), and his enjoyment of swimming, or bathing, is evident throughout his letters. He also loved to watch a good thunderstorm, as shown in the letter to Arthur Greeves quoted earlier in this chapter. In fact, Ransom's first encounter with Perelandra seems to recall that memorable experience just as does his first panorama of Malacandra. The letter to Greeves mentions a "tinkly" sound made by the distant thunder (*TST* 389), the same unusual quality Ransom notices in the Perelandrian storm.

As Lewis's imaginative re-creation of paradise, Perelandra contains an abundance of the things he associated with pleasure. From the time Ransom first splashes down in the tropical seas of the planet until he witnesses the ceremony of the Great Dance, his time spent in this world includes a good many Edenic delights: the bubble-trees, the ambrosial gourds, rides on the backs of exotic creatures. In fact, Perelandra is replete with the things Lewis himself regarded with pleasure—everything except a good book, a good smoke, and a pint of bitter.

But Perelandra also evokes a whole other species of pleasure. When Ransom, riding on a dolphin's back at night, approaches one of the floating islands, his piercing delight has an element of déjà vu.

> But he said "Hush" to his mind at this stage, for the mere pleasure of breathing in the fragrance which now began to steal towards him from the blackness ahead. Warm and sweet, and every moment sweeter and purer, and every moment stronger and more filled with all delights, it came to him. He knew well what it was, . . . the night-breath of a floating island in the star Venus. It was strange to be filled with homesickness for places where his sojourn had been so brief and which were, by any objective standard, so alien to all our race. Or were they? The cord of longing which drew him to the invisible isle seemed to him at that moment to have been fastened long, long before his coming to Perelandra, long before the earliest times that memory could recover in his childhood, before birth, before the birth of man himself, before the origins of time. It was sharp, sweet, wild, and holy, all in one. (102–3)

In this passage we see Perelandra, not only as a garden of unearthly delights, but as an image of Joy itself. The exotic garden—whether Eden, Hesperides, or Warnie's miniature garden on a biscuit tin—is one of the pictures that Lewis associated with Joy from early childhood on. The islands, too, appear throughout Lewis's books, most notably in *Pilgrim's Regress,* as a picture of unreachable paradise.

But Ransom has not come to Perelandra for his own pleasure. He has been sent on a mission not yet revealed to him. This mission does not begin on a promising note, however: the Green Lady, the Eve of Perelandra, bursts into laughter at Ransom's appearance the first time she sees him. On the voyage to Venus in a translucent casket, one side of his body has been burnt brownish red by the sun, and the other left "almost a leprous white" (55). She soon apologizes for her first reaction, but nonetheless she dubs him Piebald Man, not a very dignified sobriquet for a man sent to save a planet.

Ransom's piebald body is an image of his divided self. Though he has submitted to the will of Maleldil (God), even to the point of risking death in traveling to Perelandra, he still has within him his natural self, his own will for control, safety, and self-reliance. As shown in chapter 4, Ransom already senses an inner tension almost as soon as he begins exploring the planet: a desire to repeat all the paradisal pleasures of Perelandra counterpoised by an inner prompter warning him about clinging to such pleasures (43, 48). The tension between natural desires and this inner prompter will become more and more intense as the story unfolds. Ransom's piebald state recalls his dream in *Out of the Silent Planet,* in which he found himself straddling a garden wall—half a citizen of a fallen world, half a citizen of Deep Heaven.

Critics have applied a variety of psychological models to explain Ransom's dual nature.[11] But Ransom's inner discord here can best be understood in terms of the traditional Christian paradigms Lewis habitually drew upon—the conflict between one's sanctified self and one's natural self, between the spirit of Christ who has entered in, and the spirit of the "Old Adam" who resists the intrusion.

Even before the crisis precipitated by the arrival of Weston, Ransom's inner duality is quite apparent. When left alone by the queen of Perelandra, he experiences "Someone's Presence," creating an almost unbearable pressure upon him, squeezing out his selfhood. Gradually he learns how to deal with this overwhelming presence.

> But later on, he discovered that it was intolerable only at certain moments . . . when a man asserts his independence and feels that now at last he's on his own. When you felt like that, then the very air seemed too crowded to breathe. . . . But when you gave in to the thing, gave yourself up to it, there was no burden to be borne. It became not a load but a medium, a sort of splendour as of eatable, drinkable, breathable gold, which fed and carried you and not only poured into you but out from you as well. Taken the wrong way, it

> suffocated; taken the right way, it made terrestrial life seem, by comparison, a vacuum. (72)

Though presented in fresh and vivid imagery, what Lewis offers here is the traditional Christian teaching of finding one's freedom in submission, of discovering one's true will by surrendering to a higher will. Lewis summed up the paradox in his autobiography: "The hardness of God is kinder than the softness of men, and His compulsion is our liberation" (*SBJ* 229).

With the arrival of Weston, the serpent in this Eden, the contest over the Green Lady—and the fate of the planet—greatly intensifies Ransom's internal dissonance. Weston's philosophy has changed somewhat since his misadventures on Malacandra. Rather than the interplanetary imperialism he espoused in *Out of the Silent Planet*, he now admits of spiritual forces and sees himself as the instrument of some Universal Life Force. Apart from his philosophy, Weston serves as an intriguing projection of Ransom's inner strife.

Weston, later the Un-Man, subjects the Green Lady to arguments for disobeying Maleldil far more subtle than anything the Eve of Genesis or of *Paradise Lost* had to face. Try as he might to counteract all of these tedious arguments of insidious intent, Ransom senses that in their complex debates about discovering the true will of Maleldil, Ransom fears that "the general development was in the enemy's favour" (130).

With the Green Lady and her planet nearing a crisis, Ransom's self-doubts almost overwhelm him. "This can't go on," he thinks to himself repeatedly, as he enters into an internal debate every bit as fierce, protracted, and theologically subtle as any of his disputations with the Un-man. This dialogue between self and soul touches upon some of the most difficult questions of Christian theodicy—free will vs. determinism; the seeming absence of God; how a beneficient God could allow evil and suffering in his creation. Throughout this debate, which lasts through all of chapter 11, one side of Ransom demands some reasonable explanation for this sorry state of affairs, and the other side is willing to trust Maleldil even in the face of seeming failure. One side of him (his "voluble self") asks why Maleldil sends no miracle to save this world, why is he absent at such a critical juncture. The other side replies that his presence has been evident from the first and that the miracle he has sent is Ransom himself (141).

Nonsense, answers the voluble self: Ransom, "with his ridiculous piebald body and his ten times defeated arguments—what sort of miracle was that?" (141). Why allow the fate of a world to hinge upon the decisions of this "man of straw?" (142). The only answer to this question is that if free will is to mean anything at all, then one cannot set bounds to its consequences. If Maleldil's creatures are to be allowed meaningful choices at all, then those choices must be allowed to determine even whether worlds are to be saved or lost (142).

In the end Ransom makes his choice: to attempt to destroy the Un-man physically. Apart from the mythological dimensions of this action discussed in chapter 2, there is a psychological dimension as well. For Weston, what is left of him, is also a kind of antiself of Ransom, a projection of his own doubts and misgivings. Several times a pathetic Weston-esque voice emanates from the Un-man, not at all the pompous, unfeeling scientist, but a frightened, petulant whine uttering gibberish about fears and petty grievances stretching back to boyhood (96, 129–30, 165–71). Ransom never knows if this is a diabolic trick from the one who absorbed Weston's personhood or if it is the actual residue of Weston's decaying psyche. The question seems hardly to matter. But more important, the fearful, egocentric babblings of the Weston-voice seem uncommonly like a demented version of the complaints Ransom has been hearing from his own voluble self—the demand for an explanation, the self-pity, the tireless ego asserting its rights. In choosing to silence the Un-man once and for all, Ransom is casting his whole force of will toward the side of him who trusts in Maleldil. Once this decision had been made, Ransom finds a peace he had not yet known on this planet. On the morning he awakens resolved to do battle with the Un-man, he discovers that the piebaldness of his body has largely faded away (151).

Again risking the personal heresy, it seems possible that Weston, later the Un-man, is also a kind of shadow of Lewis's former self that he would like to excise (or exorcise) imaginatively. For example, the seemingly defeated Un-man babbles at length about his fears of Nothingness, mentioning a child who sees his grandmother's dead body and then goes off and has bad dreams (167). This recalls again Lewis's childhood trauma of having to view his mother's dead body and his lifelong nightmares.

It should be noted as well that Weston's odd combination of Bergsonian vitalism and Manichaeanism, which Lewis paints as positively demonic in *Perelandra,* recalls the author's own musings in his youth, when he was casting about for some metaphysical foundations. At the age of nineteen, Lewis had written to Arthur Greeves: "I believe in no God, least of all one who would punish me for the 'lusts of the flesh': but I do believe that I have in me a spirit, a chip, shall we say, of universal spirit; and that, since all good & joyful things are spiritual & non-material, I must be careful not to let matter (= nature = Satan, remember) get too great a hold on me" (*TST* 221). Six months later, the young Lewis explains to Greeves the theme of *Dymer,* a poem he was later to publish: "The main idea is that of development by self-destruction, both of individuals & species, as nature produces man only to conquer her [*sic*], & man produces a future & higher generation to conquer the ideals of the last" (*TST* 239). Both of these passages sound utterly unlike the Christian Lewis of later years, and they are tinged with more than a little "Westonism." It would seem that the older, reconverted Lewis writing the trilogy might have felt a special revulsion for ideas he himself had entertained in his youth, ideas he would later consider dangerous and deceptive.

In the Un-man, as well, we see a figure who would be particularly abhorrent to the author. Once Weston apparently dies and becomes "the man-aged corpse, the bogey" (*Per* 122), he seems like something straight out of a nightmare—and he probably is. Writing to Greeves in 1930, Lewis confessed that he had been troubled by dreams in which "the dead appear as bogeys." He relates in great detail a nightmare in which he dreamed he was talking to his recently deceased father when suddenly he remembered with horror that he "had been TALKING TO A DEAD MAN" (*TST* 392–93). Given this context, Ransom's task is not only to counteract all the Un-man's deceitful and insidious arguments to the Green Lady for disobeying Maleldil but to keep his nerve while arguing with the Undead. This the narrative makes plain: "For side by side with his disgust, the more childlike terror of living with a ghost or a mechanised corpse never left him for many minutes together" (129).

But in the end Ransom is able to overcome both his fears and his inner divisions. At this point he does not expect Maleldil to forestall this encounter or to supply him with supernatural powers to overcome his diabolic enemy. He has simply resolved to do his best in the battle and has no assurance of the outcome. In fact, in the middle of their combat, Ransom shouts a line from the *Battle of Maldon.* We know from more than one source what Lewis's favorite line was from this Old English poem about heroic defeat at the hands of the Danes (a sort of Anglo-Saxon version of the Battle of the Alamo). This is assuredly the line Ransom cries in the middle of this battle to the death: "Purpose shall be the firmer, heart the keener, courage shall be the more, as our might lessens."[12]

This is quite stirring and heroic—and quite unlike Ransom. Earlier in the trilogy, his temperamental habit in times of stress has been to feel betrayed by those who should have helped him but have abandoned him. In *Out of the Silent Planet,* he responds to the loneliness and danger of his trek to Augray's cave by thinking bitterly about how Weston and Devine, his fellow earthlings, ought never to have abandoned him (*OSP* 88). And the lengthy inner dialogue that fills chapter 11 of *Perelandra* centers on Ransom's feelings that Maleldil had abandoned him at his point of greatest need.

But Ransom has found a strange new courage. When he first confronts the Un-man, offering to do physical battle, the demon-corpse taunts him, playing upon his worst fears, conjuring up images of martyrs "screaming recantations too late in the middle of the fire, mouldering in concentration camps, writhing under saws, jibbering in mad-houses, or nailed on to crosses" (153).

The Ransom we have seen earlier in the trilogy might have been paralyzed by so many appalling images of annihilation and abandonment. But he stands firm in the fray and fights with unfaltering determination. Perhaps the secret of his steely resolution lies in his hearing again, quoted from memory by one who had been there, those words from the cross: *Eloi, Eloi, lama sabachthani,* "My God, my God, why hast thou forsaken me?" (153). In his letters, Lewis used Christ's sense of abandonment on the cross as an illustration to those who felt abandoned: "The Father was not *really* absent from the Son when He said 'Why hast thou forsaken me?' You see God Himself, as man, submitted to man's sense of being abandoned" (*LAL* 36–37). In his battle with the Un-man, Ransom imitates Christ's passion, setting aside fears and feelings of abandonment to complete the task given to him.

After a long sea chase and descent into a subterranean cave, the climax comes when Ransom finds Weston, accompanied by a grotesque crawling thing, another of those Wellsian abominables. Ransom assumes they are trying to frighten him, and he senses that somehow the Un-man is able to manipulate Ransom's thoughts. "Get out of my brain." Ransom cries in a rage. "It isn't yours, I tell you! Get out of it" (181). Then, invoking the Trinity, he hurls a stone at the Un-man and does away with him. In destroying the Un-man, Ransom has defeated as well that side of himself that might have prevented him from accomplishing his mission on Perelandra. (The fact that this last confrontation occurs in an underground cavern certainly reinforces one's sense that the conflict is to be seen, at one level, as a battle within the deeper reaches of the mind.) And when the battle is won, even that grotesque creature turns out to be no ally of the Un-man; he is as harmless as a pfifltriggi (182).

That Hideous Strength

In the first two books of the trilogy, Lewis clearly identifies with his protagonist Ransom. After returning from Perelandra, though, Ransom has reached a level of spiritual refinement that Lewis would never presume to have attained. Consequently, Lewis's sensibilities seem to be partially associated with a number of characters in *That Hideous Strength* but not strongly tied to any one of them. Ransom's views on male authority in marriage certainly reflect Lewis's. On the whole, however, the Ransom of *That Hideous Strength* does not resemble the author so much as he does Lewis's good friend Charles Williams (as discussed in the next chapter).

The characters of the two protagonists take something from their author. Jane Studdock's troubling dreams, her desire not to be "drawn in" (115), and her reluctant conversion (247) recall again the Lewis of *Surprised by Joy.* It is also revealing that Jane's first, epiphanic vision of Ransom makes her forget several grudges, among them her grudge against "her childhood and her father's house" (143). Mark Studdock's passion to get into the inner ring may be traced in part to Lewis's memories of his years at boarding schools and at Oxford. Life at Malvern was "wholly dominated by the social struggle," according to Lewis, where "the absorbing preoccupation" was to arrive at the top and then to remain there (*SBJ* 108). Lewis does not comment on how this atmosphere affected him personally. But when he was twenty-two, he wrote to his brother that "the real Oxford" was "a close corporation of jolly, untidy, lazy, good-for-nothing, humorous old men, who have been electing their own successors ever since the world began and who intend to go on with it." After that phrase, in which the satire thinly veils the envy, Lewis concluded by bemoaning his small chances of ever fighting his way into that "unassuming but impregnable fortress" (*LCSL* 60). Of course, the parallels here may be incidental. While Mark Studdock had "a good deal of the spaniel in him" (218), Lewis himself was always something of a contrary spirit, even in his youth, one for whom the acceptance of "we few, we happy few" would always be more important than trying to ingratiate himself with the movers and shakers of an institution.

Dr. Dimble, with his intriguing theories about Arthurian legend (31), his dread of listening to dull student papers (33), and his Christian convictions (229), seems something of a self-portrait by the author, though he is never very fully fleshed out in the story. We sense a bit of Lewis as well in Hingest's lecture to Mark on the nature of truth (70–71) and in Denniston's remark that he enjoys all kinds of weather (113; *TST* 431).

Not surprisingly, the voice of the narrator in *That Hideous Strength* also sounds very much like the author. In the description of Bragdon Wood, for example, Lewis speaks in the first person. He compares entering the wood to penetrating the holy of holies (20), then offers historical background going back to Arthurian times and adds his own thoughts about spending time alone in the wood: "I remember thinking, 'This is the sort of place which, as a child, one would have been rather afraid of or else would have liked very much indeed.' A moment later I thought, 'But when alone—really alone—everyone is a child: or no one?' Youth and age only touch the surface of our lives" (21). The interweaving here of spirituality, of medieval and other historical lore, and of the sense of the child's wonder and fear is all Lewis.

In general, though, a study of how Ransom's travels reflect Lewis's own pilgrimage must necessarily end upon Ransom's return from Perelandra. For the Ransom of *That Hideous Strength* is the pendragon and the fisher-king, not the well-intentioned but untested Pedestrian first introduced in *Out of the Silent Planet*. Ultimately it is Ransom on Perelandra that Lewis most strongly identified with. He referred to the second novel of the trilogy several times as his favorite book. And sometimes as evening fell, he was known to look up at the evening star and exclaim, "Perelandra!"

6

Models, Influences, and Echoes

> *No man who values originality will ever be original. But try to tell the truth as you see it, try to do any bit of work as well as it can be done for the work's sake, and what men call originality will come unsought.*
>
> C. S. Lewis, "Membership"

WILLIAM EMPSON described C. S. Lewis as the best-read man of his generation, one who read everything and remembered everything he read.[1] Several who knew Lewis recall that if they quoted a line from *Paradise Lost,* he could begin quoting the succeeding lines from memory.[2] In conversation or in his writing, Lewis could call to mind a passage he had seen that week or something he had read in school decades earlier. Thus in the Ransom trilogy we find interwoven with the story line not only ideas and allusions from classical mythology and the Bible but also echoes from medieval and Renaissance writers, from Icelandic myth, from science fiction and romance, and from just about any other book that might be found in Lewis's library. By studying his use of predecessor texts, one sees the kind of literary art Lewis valued most highly in other writers and discovers also his own literary art in shaping such a variety of allusions into a coherent narrative.

There are inevitable dangers in "source criticism" of an author, particularly one like Lewis. First, one's identification of antecedents or influences, however plausible, might simply be wrong. Lewis complained frequently how often critics made up fanciful histories of how he or his friends had come to compose their fiction, and he found their conjectures to be nearly always in error. He noted, for example, how many reviewers, with good reason, interpreted Tolkien's *Lord of the Rings* as an allegorical commentary on the atomic bomb. But Tolkien had completed his epic fantasy before having ever heard anything about this new and fearful weapon (*FE* 114–16).

Lewis warned of a second danger in source criticism, that of focusing so much on "getting behind the text" that one ceases to see the text itself. In "The Anthropological Approach," he argued that the power of a literary work comes from the talent and art of the author, not from the residual impact of earlier, perhaps less-known, material that the author has incorporated. For example, one does not "explain" the character of Bercilak in *Sir Gawain and the Green Knight* by saying that he is derived from a pagan vegetation god. Quite the reverse. An anthropologist who reads *Sir Gawain and the Green Knight* may learn something useful about vegetation gods, but his speculations add little to our understanding of Bercilak (*SLE* 306).

Consider an example from Lewis's own fiction: two American colleges have purchased wardrobes that Lewis owned in his lifetime, engaging occasionally in friendly skirmishes about which wardrobe is the most likely model for the one in *The Lion, the Witch, and the Wardrobe.* Visitors travel to both campuses (Wheaton College in Wheaton, Illinois, and Westmont College in Santa Barbara, California) eager to see the "real" wardrobe made famous by the *Chronicles of Narnia.* Inevitably, when they see either wardrobe, there is a letdown. After all, it is just a piece of furniture; it does not lead into Narnia. The fictional wardrobe lends enchantment to the "real" ones, not the other way around. The same often holds true for the Ransom trilogy; Lewis often illuminates his predecessor texts more than those texts illuminate our reading of Lewis.

Given these caveats, however, readers may still examine the sources and influences of the Ransom trilogy to discover its full richness of texture and meaning. It is characteristic of most creative writers that a simple phrase or image may become a kind of literary shorthand for a wealth of emotional associations or a body of ideas.

This is especially true for Lewis. As a medievalist by training, he was accustomed to reading authors who were highly syncretistic, blending classical elements with contemporary, Christian with pagan, and historical with fanciful. By temperament he was also something of an intellectual jackdaw, who took whatever ideas attracted him and "Lewisified" them.

Some readers may feel that Lewis's wide and frequent borrowing detracts from his originality. But he was unabashedly *un*original. In his address "Christianity and Literature" he notes that the most common terms of valorization in modern criticism have to do with creativity, spontaneity, or freedom from rules and conventions. Lewis summarizes the characteristic assumption: "Great authors are innovators, pioneers, explorers; bad authors bunch in schools and follow models" (*CR* 3). He contrasts this with the classical and Christian view that "an author should never conceive himself as bringing into existence beauty or wisdom that did not exist before, but simply and solely as trying to embody in terms of his own art some reflection of eternal Beauty and Wisdom" (7). In his reading of the New Testament, Lewis finds that "originality . . . is quite plainly the prerogative of God alone" and that "the art of life itself is an art of imitation" (6). He concludes, "Of every idea and of every method the Christian writer will ask not 'Is it mine?', but 'Is it good?' " (9)

One of the ironies of Lewis's life is that he should struggle mightily throughout his twenties trying to achieve greatness as a poet, to take his place among the geniuses he so admired—all to little avail. Then when he became a Christian and accepted a much humbler view of his role as an author, he launched almost immediately upon one of the most exceptional writing careers of the twentieth century.

Out of the Silent Planet

The first space-travel fantasy Lewis ever wrote is a story called "To Mars and Back." He composed it when he was five or six years old (*OOW* x). Obviously, the idea of an interplanetary voyage took hold early in Jack's fertile imagination. Left to venture at will through his parents' books, he early discovered writers like Beatrix Potter, E. Nesbit, and Jonathan Swift, who created imaginary worlds inhabited by exotic creatures.

However, Lewis's discovery of "science fiction," as usually understood, came in his schoolboy years, with his reading of H. G. Wells. Though he retained a lifelong interest in Wells, his opinion of the novelist-turned-philosopher was always mixed. At the age of fifteen, for example, Lewis wrote to Arthur Greeves, "When one has set aside the rubbish that H. G. Wells always puts in, there remains a great deal of original, thoughtful, and suggestive work in it" (*TST* 49). In another letter to Greeves four years later, Lewis admitted somewhat sheepishly that he had enjoyed reading Wells's novel *Marriage,* adding, "One thing you can say for the man is that he really is interested in all the big, outside questions" (*TST* 264). Of Wells's transition from science fiction writer to socialist philosopher, Lewis lamented that Wells had traded his birthright for a "pot of message."[3]

Yet Lewis acknowledged his debt to Wells, and when reading *Out of the Silent Planet,* one is often struck by its similarities to *First Men in the Moon.* Both stories portray a single-minded physicist who builds a spherical spaceship in his backyard, accompanied by a younger man seeking interplanetary gold; both ships make use of an arcane antigravity device; both mention the tinkling sound of meteorites on the ship's hull and the steel shutters used to shut out the intense sunlight; both show earthlings full of fears about alien worlds who, in an audience before the ruling spirit, discover that they themselves are the ones who pose a danger to other species.[4]

Despite these structural similarities, however, *Out of the Silent Planet* is fundamentally anti-Wellsian. In *Surprised by Joy* Lewis explains that his own trilogy was less a tribute to earlier science fiction than it was an exorcism of a certain coarse fascination, tinged with eroticism, which he found in the cosmic voyage narratives he had devoured in his school years (*SBJ* 35–36). He comments as well that his reading of H. G. Wells planted firmly in his boyish imagination "the vastness and cold of space, the littleness of Man" (*SBJ*

65). This is, of course, the materialist myth that Lewis deliberately seeks to subvert in the trilogy.

While writers like Wells, Stapledon, and Haldane provided the matter that Lewis wanted to respond to in *Out of the Silent Planet,* David Lindsay's *Voyage to Arcturus* showed him the method for writing what he called "theologised science fiction" (*LCSL* 260). Lindsay published a series of novels in the 1920s that reached a very small audience; in fact, he would probably be all but forgotten today if Lewis had not praised him "as the real father of my planet books."[5] Lewis wrote to the American scholar Charles A. Brady that *Voyage* first gave him "the idea that the 'scientifiction' appeal could be combined with the 'supernatural' appeal" (*LCSL* 205). He explained more fully to his friend Ruth Pitter: "From Lindsay I first learned what other planets in fiction are really good for; for *spiritual* adventures. Only they can satisfy the craving which sends our imaginations off the earth. Or putting it another way, in him I first saw the terrific results produced by the union of two kinds of fiction hitherto kept apart; the Novalis, G. Macdonald, James Stephens sort and the H. G. Wells, Jules Verne sort. My debt to him is very great."[6]

Such high praise has encouraged some readers of Lewis to turn to Lindsay's *Voyage to Arcturus,* hoping to find there the inventive and adventurous plot of Wells and Verne blended with the otherworldliness and spirituality of Morris and Macdonald. Instead they are likely to find a rather repellent and awkwardly structured tale in which the quest for truth and goodness ends only in a maze of illusions and a sense that good and evil are one and the same.

Lewis himself was not at all attracted to the theme of *Voyage to Arcturus.* In fact, he pronounced the book "on the borderline of the diabolical . . . [and] so manichean as to be almost satanic."[7] (Indeed, Harold Bloom has noted that "no other fictional work inflicts such spiritual violence upon its audience").[8] Yet Lindsay proved that the cosmic voyage could be more than just an adventure story; it could become a vehicle for serious philosophical exploration. Lewis praised the novel for its "lived dialectic," the way its twists and turns in plot reflect successive attempts to arrive at some final truth, each one to be undercut by some new development in the story (*OOW* 12).

Throughout *Voyage to Arcturus,* the inner lives of the story's characters are also revealed by their outer shapes. For example, when Maskull, the protagonist, first awakens on Tormance, a planet circling Arcturus, he discovers that his body has been changed; there is a protuberance on his forehead, a lump on his neck beneath each ear, and a tentacle growing out of his chest. Soon he learns that these seeming disfigurements are actually new organs—to give him powers of telepathy, empathy, and magnanimity that he lacked on earth. Thus Lindsay uses the fantasy convention of alien creatures with exotic anatomies to depict, perhaps a bit heavy-handedly, his characters and theme. The feature of *Voyage* that made the deepest impression on Lewis was Lindsay's creation of plausible physical details that are also imbued with psychological and spiritual significance.

Another writer whose influence is most apparent in *Out of the Silent Planet* is Jonathan Swift. Ransom's encounter with the ideal community of the hrossa and his interview with the Oyarsa bear a number of similarities to Gulliver's experiences in part 4 of *Gulliver's Travels,* "A Voyage to the Country of the Houyhnhnms." The word *hross* is Old Norse for "horse," and the persistent initial *h* in the hrossa's speech reminds us as well of the neighing speech of Swift's creations.

Jeannette Hume Lutton has best summarized the structural similarities between the two stories.

> Both [protagonists] find themselves in fantastic surroundings as the result of treachery and violence at the hands of their fellow men. Both, wandering friendless and unprovisioned in a totally unknown environment, encounter rational beings whom they initially take to be beasts. Both recognize the rationality of these creatures by hearing them talk. Both go home with the creatures they have met, live for a considerable time among them, learn their language, communicate something of the cultures they represent to their hosts . . . and learn something of the host culture, grow to love and admire their hosts but eventually find themselves under the necessity of leaving them, and after further adventures, return to their own lands

> with changed outlook and a kind of permanent homesickness for the culture that once seemed so alien.[9]

To this overall summary one can add incidental parallels such as the surprise of the alien creatures when they discover that the protagonist's clothes are not part of his natural covering and their disgust when they hear the sorry history of our own species. In a conversation with Brian Aldiss and Kingsley Amis, Lewis agreed that a modern-day Swift would probably send his Gulliver to some other planet, a position that has encouraged readers to look for Swiftian touches in the Ransom trilogy (*OOW* 143).

Apart from speculating about literary sources for *Out of the Silent Planet,* critics have also shown a great deal of interest in possible real-life models for the main characters in the story. As explained in chapter 5, the character of Ransom seems to be largely created in the image of his maker. Some scholars, though, have compared Ransom to Tolkien, whose specialty was languages.[10] However, Tolkien did not think Ransom was modeled on himself, though he saw in Ransom some of his own ideas "Lewisified."[11] And Lewis explained that he made Ransom a philologist because the plot would require someone who could acquire new languages quickly.[12]

Other readers see a great deal of Charles Williams in the character of Ransom, especially as he appears in *That Hideous Strength.* This is undoubtedly true. But Lewis had not yet met Williams when he wrote *Out of the Silent Planet,* so his initial conception could not have been based on Williams. It would appear that when Lewis presents his protagonist as a soul-in-progress, Ransom most resembles Lewis himself. But once Ransom has overcome the major spiritual challenges facing him, from within and without, once he has achieved the status of pendragon, he comes more to resemble Charles Williams, someone Lewis greatly admired for the quality of holiness in his life.

There has been a wealth of speculation by Lewis's critics and biographers about possible sources for the characters of Devine and Weston. J. B. S. Haldane is most often named as the model for Weston. Certainly, some of Weston's ideas in *Out of the Silent Planet* sound like Haldane's sentiments in *Possible Worlds,* especially the defense of research on animals and the vision of our species reaching out to fill the galaxy. But Haldane's books show a healthy appreciation for the arts and the humanities, which one cannot picture him dismissing, like Weston, as "unscientific foolery" (*OSP* 13). Lewis himself said that Weston is a composite (*OOW* 78), and the books of the trilogy bear him out on this. In this book and in *Perelandra,* Weston's speeches strongly echo not only Haldane but also Stapledon, Wells, Shaw, Bergson, and other proponents of Evolutionism. Note, for example, the closing words of Weston's speech to the Oyarsa: "What lies in the future, beyond our present ken, passes imagination to conceive: it is enough for me that there is a Beyond" (*OSP* 137). This sentence reminds us of the passage quoted above from Haldane's "Man's Destiny," but the closing words are also nearly identical to those found in Shaw's *Back to Methuselah* (1921): "It is enough that there is a beyond."

Devine is probably also a composite, though he is most often associated with T. D. ("Harry") Weldon, a philosophy tutor at Lewis's college at Oxford and his nemesis.[13] Weldon was a progressive and a free thinker, and he and Lewis took opposite sides, not only in philosophical matters, but also in the college's political affrays. At some points their relationship became so strained that they were barely on speaking terms.[14] Lewis particularly disliked Weldon's arrogance in debate, his deliberate rudeness such as we see in Feverstone's treatment of Canon Jewel and others (*DCSL* 445). If Weldon really were the model for Devine, then Lewis's satire here is especially pointed; he gives Weldon's nickname, Harry, to the half-witted boy whom Devine tries to kidnap before deciding to take Ransom instead.

Ironically, Weldon was the "hard-boiled atheist" mentioned in *Surprised by Joy* (224) who told Lewis that the historical credibility of the Gospels was surprisingly good, that the Dying God myth seemed actually to have happened once. That certainly seems an unlikely remark to come from the mouth of a hard-boiled atheist. Martin Moynihan, who was a student of both Weldon and Lewis, has argued that Weldon seemed somewhere between agnosticism and deism, rather than militant atheism.[15] Moynihan records a number of cryptic remarks Weldon made about theology and morality that tend to make one think that Lewis's characterization of him as an atheist is a bit overstated.

However, it would be a mistake to associate Devine too closely with Weldon. After all, the latter was an academic and a trained philosopher, one whose intellectual credentials Lewis seemed to assume with a begrudging respect. Devine, on the other hand, is a breezy man of the world, an intellectual dilettante whose only interest lies in getting ahead (though he was elected to a fellowship under mysterious circumstances). One cannot imagine Devine, even for a moment, stopping to consider the historicity of the Gospels or the nature of morality. His natural milieu is not a university town but London.

In fact, Devine is the incarnation of the values that Lewis associated with boyhood. Lewis explains that Ransom felt for Devine "that sort of distaste we feel for someone whom we have admired in boyhood for a very brief time and then outgrown" (*OSP* 15). Devine had entertained his schoolfellows "with that kind of humour which consists in a perpetual parody of the sentimental or idealistic clichés of one's elders" (15). His flippancy and cynicism, his worldly and sophisticated air, the "varnished vulgarity" of his speech all remind us of the young man Lewis calls Pogo in *Surprised by Joy*, the one who made the young Lewis aspire to be "a fop, a cad, and a snob" (68). Lewis's depiction of Devine bears a number of resemblances to his description of Pogo, even to the repetition of key words such as "flashy" and "gentleman" (*OSP* 15; *SBJ* 17). Of course, Pogo was just out of university, and Devine is approaching middle age. But for those who never outgrow boyhood, the years hardly matter: "As far as Ransom could gather from their brief conversation in the yard, his old schoolfellow had altered very little" (*OSP* 15).

Perelandra

The two most obvious sources of *Perelandra* are the first three chapters of Genesis and Milton's *Paradise Lost*. As discussed in chapter 2, the Green Lady is naked and unashamed like the prelapsarian Eve, and she is tempted like Eve, though fortunately with different results.

Lewis probably first got the idea for *Perelandra* while working on his *Preface to Paradise Lost.* Margaret P. Hannay has shown that Lewis retained in *Perelandra* the elements of *Paradise Lost* that he most admired, while altering the elements he found fault with in Milton. Lewis considered Milton's Satan to be too impressive in the early books, so he made the tempter of the Green Lady entirely contemptible; he thought that Milton was mistaken in trying to portray God directly, so that Maleldil is only an elusive but powerful presence on Perelandra; he thought that Milton erred in trying to show human sexuality before the Fall, so he keeps the king and queen apart for most of the story; finally he rewrites the ending so that a second Fall may be averted.[16]

Apart from its broad narrative outlines, *Perelandra* is indebted to *Paradise Lost* for a great many details of characterization and setting. For instance, Lewis approved of the regal demeanor with which Milton invested the first pair (*PPL* 119), and he heightens this element in his Eden story. Also, the Green Lady's momentary disappointment when she sees Ransom and recognizes that it is not her husband (68) parallels Eve's initial disappointment when she first sees Adam and does not consider him as fair as her own reflection in a pool (4, 477–91). And when the Un-man scorns Ransom and boasts that he is of a much higher order of creation than the human (119), he echoes the fallen Satan contemptuously telling the angels who guard Eve that once they were no peers of his (4, 27–34).

The other masterpiece of English poetry whose influence is most apparent in *Perelandra* is Spenser's *Faerie Queene.* The descriptions of the floating islands as paradisal gardens recall the Garden of Adonis (bk. 3), and Lewis's depiction of the dragon and tree with golden apples closely resembles Spenser's Hesperides. As shown in chapter 4, Lewis's floating islands reverse the moral valence of Spenser's Wandering Islands (bk. 3), which are unsafe places where true knights should not dally. *The Faerie Queene* may also have provided Lewis with the idea of having people travel through oceans on the backs of dolphins, though that tradition is older than Spenser.

In Lewis's lectures on *The Faerie Queene,* he points out several motifs in the poem that reappear in his own *Perelandra.* He mentions, for example, medieval and Renaissance speculations that "aquatic elemental spirits" may actually exist, then adds cryptically, "and who knows, perhaps in this as in so many things the ancients knew more than we" (*SIL* 129). Whether or not mermen and mermaids exist in the earth's oceans, they do in Perelandra's (161–62). Lewis also mentions the Renaissance love of literary pageants as found in Spenser (*SIL* 127), and then he presents a splendid modern specimen in the Great Dance sequence at the end of *Perelandra.* Lastly, it is interesting to note that Lewis interprets the episode in which Florimell is held captive in a dark cave (bk. 3) as "very like an allegory of the descent of the soul into material embodiment" (*SIL* 126). As discussed in chapter 2, Lewis's description of Ransom's descent into the subterranean cavern in *Perelandra* is intriguingly similar to his comparison of the Incarnation to a deep-sea diver in *Miracles.* Lewis's reading of Florimell's captivity suggests that the image in both books is derived from Spenser.

Lewis's borrowing from more recent writers cannot be demonstrated with any certainty. Green and Hooper suggest that the idea of floating islands on Venus may have come from a phrase in Olaf Stapledon's *First and Last Men* about "great floating islands of vegetable matter."[17] Donald Glover speculates that the contest between Ransom and Weston over the will of the Green Lady may be rooted in another scene in *First and Last Men* in which an American emissary and a Chinese emissary compete over a naked native woman from another planet.[18] C. N. Manlove, in his turn, asserts that "without a doubt" Lewis got his image of the island paradise from a little book called *Melmoth the Wanderer* published in 1820.[19] But there are so many pictures of an island paradise for Lewis to draw upon—Hesperides, Avalon, Tirnanog, and others—that readers need not assume his imagination was fed by only one spring.

That Hideous Strength

That Hideous Strength is longer than *Out of the Silent Planet* and *Perelandra* combined, and it probably draws on a greater variety of sources, personal and literary, than the other two combined. Critics have both praised and criticized the book for its panoply of characters, images, and motifs, and a survey of Lewis's sources does indeed reveal the range and diversity of sources he has woven into the narrative.

The person who exerted the greatest influence on the composition of *That Hideous Strength* is Charles Williams. In fact, the third novel of the trilogy has been jocularly described as "a Charles Williams novel written by C. S. Lewis."[20] Williams had written to Lewis in 1936 praising Lewis's literary history *The Allegory of Love* at just the same time Lewis wrote to Williams praising his fantasy *The Place of the Lion.* When Williams moved to Oxford in 1939, the two developed a deep friendship, and Williams became a regular member of the Inklings.

Though he was a prolific writer, Williams is mainly remembered for his novels, dubbed "spiritual thrillers," and for his Arthurian poems, *Taliessen through Logres* and *The Region of the Summer Stars.* His novels were usually set in contemporary England, but an England haunted by what he called "Arch-natural" forces. In *War in Heaven* the Holy Grail turns up in the hands of a country archdeacon; in *Many Dimensions* a magical stone appears in the middle of London; in *Greater Trumps* the eternal dance of the universe is reflected in a pack of tarot cards. Though Williams was a Christian, he had an unusual fascination for the occult, and the sorcerers and black magicians in his stories seem to be portrayed with as much zest as his good characters. Two of the recurrent motifs in Williams's stories are the interpenetration of different time frames and the use or abuse of power.[21]

Lewis's depiction of all the unprincipled characters and occult machinations at N.I.C.E. certainly owes something to Williams's fascination with depraved characters and their black arts. The return of Merlin to the twentieth century is also something one might expect to find in Williams. The character of Ransom as portrayed in *That Hideous Strength* somewhat resembles Williams as well. Jane's world is transformed when she meets Ransom's, and she has such a strong sense of his sanctity that she literally sees him with a halo at one point (278). Lewis was similarly impressed by Williams, whom he described as having "the face of an angel" when he spoke (*EPCW* ix.) (His response was not atypical; T. S. Eliot and W. H. Auden also spoke of Williams as if he were a living saint.)[22] Even though Williams was not a handsome man, he attracted the admiration of a number of young married women, whom he advised, as Ransom does Jane, that they could best express their feelings for him by channeling their love back to their husbands (*LCSL* 208).

Williams is also quoted directly in *That Hideous Strength.* When MacPhee declares that they ought to be moving against the forces gathering at N.I.C.E., Camilla Denniston answers by quoting a line from *Taliessen through Logres:* "All lies in a passion of patience, my lord's rule" (194). In Williams's poem "Mount Badon," the restive Taliessen wants to attack the Saxons, but he is counseled, in the line above, to the effect that they also serve who only stand and wait. The next day Arthur, Taliessen, and the other Britons defeat the Saxons, stemming the tide of the invasion. So Camilla's quotation here is not only exhortatory but prophetic.

Lewis read all three books of the trilogy at meetings of his informal literary club, the Inklings, and sometimes he gives the impression that he did not want to leave any of his listeners out of the story. He explains in the preface of *That Hideous Strength* that references to Atlantis as Numinor and the True West (272) come from an unpublished manuscript by his friend J. R. R. Tolkien, the work later published as the *The Lord of the Rings.* One might suppose that Tolkien would be flattered by the acknowledgment, but Tolkien generally treated Lewis's little borrowings not as a tribute but as plagiarism.[23] He explained that the term should be spelled *Numenor* (Elvish for "West-land"), not *Numinor,* a word Lewis probably connected in his mind with "numinous." Tolkien also conjectured that Lewis's "eldils" were derived from his "Eldar" and that the names for the king and queen of Perelandra, Tor and Tinidril, were influenced by two of his characters, Tuor and Idril.[24]

Lewis's friend Owen Barfield, referred to in *Perelandra* as an anthroposophist called B. (32), is referred to by name in *That Hideous Strength.* While the others are out in the rain trying to locate the newly awakened Merlin, MacPhee and Ivy Maggs fall into a debate about whether animals can experience emotions, such as friendship, or whether they behave merely out of physical needs. Ransom calls this a false distinction, saying that there is a unity of needs and feelings in animals, "one of Barfield's 'ancient unities' " (261).

This seems like an incidental allusion, and certainly the issue under discussion has no great implications for the story as a whole. But Barfield's paradigm of ancient unities greatly influenced Lewis's thought, helping shape his views on language, theology, and cultural history. Lewis explains the meaning of the phrase more fully in *Miracles,* where he alludes to Barfield's *Poetic Diction.*

> Mr. Barfield has shown, as regards the history of language, that words did not start by referring merely to physical objects and then get extended by metaphor to refer to emotions, mental states and the like. On the contrary, what we now call the "literal and metaphorical" meanings have both been disengaged by analysis from an ancient unity of meaning which was neither or both. In the same way it is quite erroneous to think that man started with a "material" God or "Heaven" and gradually spiritualised them. . . . He started with something which was neither and both. As long as we are trying to read back into that ancient unity either the one or the other of the two opposites which have since been analysed out of it, we shall misread all early literature and ignore many states of consciousness which we ourselves still from time to time experience. (79)

Given Lewis's theory of language discussed in chapter 4, he would be highly attracted to a primal tongue that could be at once concrete (literal) and abstract (metaphoric). His "Old Solar," spoken in Deep Heaven and on unfallen planets, is intended to be just such a language that preserves the ancient unities. The very speaking of Old Solar betokens a unified consciousness that humans do not have. When Dimble practices in the Great Tongue what he will say to Merlin when they find him, Jane does not understand the words, but she grasps their essence: "The voice did not sound like Dimble's own: it was as if the words spoke themselves through him from some strong place at a distance—or as if they were not words at all but present operations of God, the planets, and the Pendragon. For this was the language spoken before the Fall and beyond the Moon and the meanings were not given to the syllables by chance, or skill, or long tradition, but truly inherent in them as the shape of the great Sun is inherent in the little waterdrop. This was Language itself" (228–29).

Apart from its implications for language, the idea that ancient unities have become bifurcated informs Dr. Dimble's discussion with his wife about the universe coming to a point. He says that minds are getting more and more spiritual and matter getting more and more material and that in literature prose and poetry are drawing further apart (284). He also suspects that there were "neutrals" in the Middle Ages, creatures such as gods, elves, dwarfs, and water people who were neither good nor evil; they were simply what they were. But as the universe comes to a point, there is no room for these neutrals, only those who stand with Maleldil or against him (285). There is a good deal of Lewis in Dr. Dimble's conjectures here, a wistful Lewis wondering if the creatures described in *The Discarded Image* might have existed once in an ancient, less centrifugal, age. Dr. Dimble's speculations about ancient unities cast a wide net. Lewis complained that the term *Renaissance* created a contrived entity out of heterogeneous cultural events (*EL* 55); one might make the same charge about the sweeping generalizations grouped together by Dr. Dimble in this passage.

Just as the organization at N.I.C.E. illustrates the syndrome described in Lewis's essay "The Inner Ring," the gathering at St. Anne's represents Lewis's ideal of community as developed in his essay "Membership," originally published the same year as *That Hideous Strength*. In "Membership," Lewis advises his readers not to respond to the dehumanizing effects of modern collectivism by retreating into an isolated individualism. Rather they should seek to become members in a mystical community, acting like bodily organs that are different in structure and function yet that work in a complementary fashion to sustain the whole (*FE* 15; this metaphor is taken from 1 Corinthians 12). Lewis notes that a man may lose his name in prison, the collectivist extreme, but also in a family, where he is simply known by his role, Father (17).

At St. Anne's each man and woman, even the beasts of the household, are members of the "company," a term for mystical community that Lewis borrowed from Williams's Arthurian books. MacPhee, the resident skeptic, is a reminder of Lewis's old tutor Kirkpatrick. Both are portrayed as dour logic-choppers who are funny without meaning to be, but both insist on clear thinking, a trait that Lewis obviously admired. George Sayer noted that Lewis describes both as having coarse hands.[25] Jane Studdock may take her name from Jane McNeill, the member of a Belfast family whom Lewis had known since childhood and for whom he always retained a great deal of affection (*TST* 69). *That Hideous Strength* is dedicated "To J. McNeill," and Lewis asked in a letter to Greeves if it mattered that his heroine in the book had the same name as the person to whom it was dedicated (*TST* 499–50).

The names of several other characters at St. Anne's serve to reinforce the author's themes. Lewis wrote that one of the central conflicts in *That Hideous Strength* is "Nature against Anti-Nature."[26] At St. Anne's, a community living close to nature, we find characters with names such as Ivy, Camilla, and Miss Ironwood. At N.I.C.E., in contrast, the names suggest hardness, artificiality, or anti-nature: Steele, Hardcastle, Feverstone, Frost, and Wither.

The animals at St. Anne's seemed to have been named not for any thematic purpose but simply for their amusing literary associations. Mr. Bultitude is named after the self-satisfied father in F. Anstey's fantasy *Vice Versa* (1882), who finds he has a lot to learn when he and his son change places. Lewis always enjoyed the book, calling it "the only truthful school story in existence" (*SBJ* 41). (Perhaps too he delighted in the idea of turning the tables on his own father?) Jack and his brother dubbed a rather comical bear at the Whipsnade Zoo outside Oxford as Mr. Bultitude (*LCSL* 153–54).

Baron Corvo (Latin "crow"), the jackdaw, takes his name from the nom de plume of Frederick W. Rolfe, whose novel *Hadrian the Seventh* (1904) Lewis and Warren found highly entertaining (*TST* 469).

Biographers and critics have offered a variety of speculations about source materials for Merlin in *That Hideous Strength.* In Dr. Dimble's impromptu lecture on the cultural underpinnings of Arthurian legend (*THS* 31), he mentions the twelfth-century English poet Layamon. J. A. W. Bennett recalls that in Lewis's own lectures on Layamon's *Brut,* the selections Lewis read aloud focused on Merlin.[27] Indeed, the Merlin of the *Brut,* like the Merlin in *That Hideous Strength,* is a shaggy, half-savage man who gives fealty only to the pendragon, who challenges his rivals by asking them riddling questions, and who demands that his enemies be beheaded. A. N. Wilson suspects that Lewis's Merlin is influenced as well by his recollections of W. B. Yeats.[28] In his early twenties, Lewis had attended a kind of literary seance in Yeats's rooms and come away impressed by Yeats's imposing physical presence, his awe-inspiring eloquence, and his familiarity with magic (*LCSL* 56–57). Roger Lancelyn Green and Walter Hooper also sense the influence of Yeats and note that Jane's dream of Merlin sleeping in a vault beneath Bragdon Wood strongly resembles a scene in E. L. Arnold's *Lepidus the Centurion.*[29]

Some of the characters at N.I.C.E. also seem to have their literary precursors. Filostrato, the scientist who would like to have all organic life wiped off the planet (172–76), probably takes his name from Philostratus, a third-century Greek philosopher. In *English Literature in the Sixteenth Century, Excluding Drama,* Lewis describes Philostratus as one of the earliest theorists to assert that art was not an imitation of nature but a representation of Platonic forms; thus art could sometimes be superior to nature and need not confine itself to the limits imposed by nature (320). Filostrato's preference of metal trees over natural ones (*THS* 172) derives perhaps from the metallic vegetation in Spenser's Bower of Bliss, which Lewis interpreted as an emblem of decadence and sterile artifice (*AL* 324–25).

Filostrato, who wants to produce Mind liberated from organic life (172), has gotten as far as keeping a head alive without its body—or so he thinks. The idea of a living, bodiless head could have come from a number of sources. As mentioned above in chapter 4, Lewis had read of a German experiment to keep a dog's head alive. (Note Miss Ironwood's mention [195] of a similar experiment by a German.) Writing during World War II, Lewis, with his images of Germans and Italians engaging in revolting medical experiments, would certainly strike a chord in British and American readers. There is also a superbrain kept alive by biomedical apparatus in Stapledon's *First and Last Men,* the book that Lewis mentions in the preface of *That Hideous Strength* as one he is responding to. But as early as 1923 Lewis himself had contemplated writing a horror story about a corpse kept alive by scientists (*DCSL* 238) and in 1930 he reported to Arthur Greeves a vivid nightmare about finding a severed head (*TST* 377). So his imagination anticipated many of the grotesqueries that he read about in later years.

There is some disagreement about the model for Jules, the spokesperson, or "mascot," of N.I.C.E. Mark Hillegas treats Jules as a caricature of H. G. Wells, one who popularizes scientism without really being a qualified scientist.[30] Roger Lancelyn Green emphatically disagrees with this identification, explaining that Lewis knew Wells only through his books and had no motive for ridiculing him personally. Green adds that Lewis once told him that Green's earlier book on space voyages was too hard on Wells and that Lewis felt no personal animosity toward him.[31] Joe R. Christopher is not convinced, noting that Jules—like Wells—is a Cockney, a popular journalist, an epicurean, and someone whose science is out of date in his later years.[32] One might add that one of Wells's most polemical works, *The Science of Life* (1929), was coauthored by Julian Huxley. "Jules" could be a portmanteau word based upon "Julian" and "Wells."

Green and Hooper suggest that the institute itself, located at Belbury, may be derived in part from a controversy over the founding of an atomic factory near Blewbury, fifteen miles outside of Oxford. They also note that the scene in which Belbury is destroyed borrows from George Bottomly's poem "Babel,"[33] an apt source for a denouement in which those who try to become gods lose even their natural human powers.

It can be seen that the books of the trilogy draw upon a vast array of sources—autobiographical, literary, and philosophical. One of the pleasures of reading *Out of the Silent Planet, Perelandra,* and *That Hideous Strength* is to discover Lewis's artful blend of disparate materials into coherent narratives bound together by a single overarching vision. In *Out of the Silent Planet* a Wellsian plot structure is used to reveal a medieval cosmology. In *Perelandra* Miltonic epic is reshaped as fantasy of the William Morris variety. In *That Hideous Strength* academic satire such as we might find in Kingsley Amis is juxtaposed to Arthurian legend. Though some critics have found the books of the trilogy, especially the last one, overly full, none would deny Lewis's prodigious reading or his remarkable powers of synthesis.

7

The Achievement of C. S. Lewis: Assessing the Trilogy

MARK R. HILLEGAS, who has written two influential books on science fiction and fantasy, wrote in 1960 that "many would agree that in C. S. Lewis's trilogy science fiction has up to now reached its highest level as literature."[1] In contrast, the poet and novelist John Wain, who was a student of Lewis, dismissed the trilogy four years later in two words: "simply bad."[2] Most assessments of Lewis's achievement in the trilogy fall somewhere in between. *Out of the Silent Planet, Perelandra,* and *That Hideous Strength* are widely praised for their intellectual vigor, for their mythopoeic qualities, and for the fluency and vividness of Lewis's prose style. Negative commentary about the trilogy has tended to focus on a few key issues: effectiveness of characterization, an anti-scientific bias, sexism or even misogyny, and inappropriate violence.

One of Lewis's most eloquent critics was J. B. S. Haldane, the scientist whose ideas Lewis caricatured in the crackbrained visions of Weston. In 1946 Haldane published a witty and acerbic review of the trilogy entitled "Auld Hornie F. R. S.," which charged that Lewis did not know science well enough to write convincing science fiction; that he was too contemptuous of science and scientists to have any real influence on them; and that he reduced complex moral, social, and political problems to simple choices between good and evil, between God and the devil. Lewis makes himself a useful prop for the existing social order, says Haldane, because he denounces scientific planning as hellish and reduces political issues to matters of piety. Haldane's arguments are incisive and entertainingly expressed—though his credibility with many contemporary readers suffers when he concludes the review by saying that the real salvation of humanity comes not from Christianity but from Communism: "For Mammon has been cleared off a sixth of our planet's surface, and his realm is contracting in Europe today. It was men, not angels, who cast him out."[3]

Lewis composed a rejoinder to Professor Haldane but did not submit it for publication. Found among his papers after his death, Lewis's "Reply to Professor Haldane" addresses several of the criticisms most often raised by reviewers and critics of the trilogy. Lewis begins by correcting one of Haldane's own errors, demonstrating that medieval scientists had a more accurate picture of the earth than Haldane claimed they did. "In other words," observes Lewis, "the Professor is about as good a historian as I am a scientist. The difference is that his false history is produced in works intended to be true, whereas my false science is produced in romances" (*OOW* 76). Such a palpable hit in his opening remarks shows what a formidable opponent Lewis must have been in debate.

Lewis goes on to explain that the books of the trilogy are "fantasies" and "romances," with only enough science to create a willing suspension of disbelief in the average reader (*OOW* 76). His comments on genre here are revealing, because they show that readers judging the trilogy as "science fiction novels" are not reading, as Pope advised, "in the same spirit that the author writ." Science fiction and fantasy are generally regarded as separate genres: science fiction stays within the bounds of physical laws as presently understood, seeking to establish plausibility for the extraordinary. Fantasy is bound only by the laws of imagination and simply presents the extraordinary as a given. Science fiction writers may feel obligated to offer explanations for interstellar travel, time travel, or other matters behind the reach of today's science. Fantasy writers, in contrast, simply present talking rabbits, witches, or hobbits as part of their imagined world.

In the trilogy Lewis makes plain his intent to break down the barriers between myth and history, and he seems to intermix genres as well. *Out of the Silent Planet* begins as if it is science fiction. But

Weston offers a rather feeble explanation that his spaceship can fly by "exploiting the less observed properties of solar radiation" (26). And Lewis's pictures of outer space and of Mars are clearly based on medieval cosmology, popular traditions, and his own imagination, not upon the best scientific data available when he wrote. *Perelandra* is more clearly a fantasy from the start. When Ransom announces that he will travel to Venus in a coffin-shaped casket, his friend "Lewis" asks all the questions a science fiction reader would want to know: how will he be propelled? how will he breathe and eat? and so on. Ransom dispenses with all this and says he will simply be carried to Venus by the Oyarsa of Malacandra (27). (Readers who find this contrived should remember that, in the medieval universe, one of the responsibilities of each planetary intelligence is to carry that world and keep it in its proper path.) Aware of the possibilities of genre confusion in *That Hideous Strength,* Lewis calls it in the subtitle "A Modern Fairy-Tale for Grown-Ups."

When Lewis calls his stories "romances," "tall stories," and "fairy-tales," it becomes clear that he has some other kind of prose fiction in mind than the novel as usually understood. Further clarification of his intentions in the trilogy may be found in his own commentaries on genre. In *Spenser's Images of Life* (composed by Alastair Fowler from Lewis's lecture notes), the novel is distinguished from other kinds of storytelling: "The novel calls for characters with insides; but there are other kinds of narrative that do not. . . . In literature, the narrative forms that do without character are quite numerous. They include, for example, the ballad, the Märchen, the adventure story, and the myth" (*SIL* 113–14). Lewis adds chivalric romance like Spenser's to his list of narrative forms that do not require psychological complexity and then enunciates a general principle about the relationship between plot and character: "The more ordinary and probable the external story is, the more it should have fully studied characters. Obversely, the more phantasmagoric the external story, the less 'inside' its characters should have" (114).

Since Lewis referred to the books of his trilogy as romances, fairy-tales, and "thrillers," it is clear that he would apply the above principles of narratology to his own fiction. Readers who object to implausible scientific details or to two-dimensional characters are not following Henry James's advice to grant the author his donnée. Some more recent critics have come to Lewis's fantasy works with more informed genre expectations than did earlier readers. For example, J. R. Christopher in *C. S. Lewis* (1987) offers an excellent discussion of the conventions of romance that apply to the trilogy.[4]

The question remains why Lewis was drawn to genres that did not require characters with "insides." One answer would be that he tended to view things in black-and-white terms—"we few" against the world. There is certainly some truth in this. The besetting weakness of a person of strong convictions may often be a certain narrowness of sympathies, a suspicion of people who do not share those convictions. Most of the characters in the trilogy are clearly on Our Side or on the Other Side. And those on the Other Side are not presented for the purposes of character study; rather, each one represents a dangerous idea or a moral failing.

In a sense, the secondary characters in the trilogy function more as a part of the setting than as independent entities; their importance lies mainly in how they affect the consciousness of the central intelligence from whose point of view the story is being told (Ransom in *Out of the Silent Planet* and *Perelandra,* Mark and Jane Studdock in *That Hideous Strength*). Again, Lewis's comments on earlier romances illuminate his own narrative technique. Referring to the plot construction of *King Solomon's Mines* and *The Wind in the Willows,* Lewis compares them to musical compositions.

> A story of this kind is in a way more like a symphony than a novel. Corresponding to the themes of the musical form, the literary form has images, which may be delicious or threatening or cryptic or grotesque, but which are always richly expressive of mood. The images are in every possible relation of contrast, mutual support, development, variation, half-echo, and the like, just as the musical themes are. But the ostensible connection between them all—what keeps the meddling intellect quiet—is here provided by the fact that they are all *happening* to someone. They are all worked into the experience of the world of the characters "whose" story it is. That, no more and no less, is the *raison d'être* of the characters in the characterless story. (*SIL* 116)

It seems clear that Lewis attempted to apply the method of *King Solomon's Mines* and *The Wind in the Willows* to the writing of the trilogy when he explains the structure of *Perelandra* in terms of Wagnerian opera (*LCSL* 205) or when he compares "The Descent of the Gods" chapter in *That Hideous Strength* to Holst's *The Planets* (*LCSL* 209).

Besides complaints about flat characters in the trilogy, reviewers and critics have often echoed Haldane in commenting on what seems to be Lewis's habitual aversion for science and scientists. In his "Reply to Professor Haldane," Lewis disagrees that the main targets of his satire in the trilogy are scientists. He notes that the one real scientist in *That Hideous Strength* is murdered because he wants to leave N.I.C.E. once he has discovered that its work is not really about science (*OOW* 78). Rather Lewis identifies his real targets as "scientism" and collectivism. Scientism, according to Lewis, is the quasi-religious hope of using technology to perpetuate the species on other worlds and to grope toward godhood (*OOW* 76–77). Lewis found this philosophy articulated less often by actual scientists than by scientific popularizers like Wells and Stapledon. Lewis concludes his reply by saying he intended the trilogy as a cautionary tale against totalitarians who use "scientific planning" as their catchphrase to attract popular support. He says that the underlying theme of *That Hideous Strength* is not, as Haldane claims, "that scientific planning will certainly lead to hell," but rather the converse that "under modern conditions any effective invitation to hell will certainly appear in the guise of scientific planning—as Hitler's regime in fact did" (*OOW* 80). It is not the sciences themselves, according to Lewis, that pose the danger but those who would use the prestige of science and the power of the state to impose an "ideological oligarchy" (80). These are the views expressed more fully in *The Abolition of Man*.

Lewis's self-defense is partly convincing on this point. Indeed, most of the degenerate characters at N.I.C.E. are managers and technocrats, not research scientists. And Lewis does show a trained scientist as a part of the company at St. Anne's (though he is the least attractive member of the group—partly because of his overbearing, no-nonsense scientific manner). But there does seem to be an excessively sweeping condemnation of technology in the trilogy. In *Out of the Silent Planet* Ransom is embarrassed to report to the hrossa all the "wars and industrialisms" (70) that have plagued earth, as if the two are twin curses. In *Perelandra,* space travel is treated as a breaking of Maleldil's quarantine, a spreading of earth's corruption to other worlds (81). Indeed, when Lewis heard rumors of actual plans for space travel, he commented acerbically, "I begin to be afraid that the villains will really contaminate the moon (*LCSL* 210). In *That Hideous Strength* modern technology seems to be almost totally in the hands of those leading a vast global conspiracy to rob humans of their personhood.

Readers of the trilogy will not be surprised to learn that Lewis was "fearful of the internal combustion engine";[5] that he preferred walking to riding in a car, because riding in a vehicle "annihilates space" (*SBJ* 157); that he disliked newspapers, cinema, radio, and television;[6] and that he seldom carried a pocketwatch or a pen.[7] So there does seem to be some truth in the charge that Lewis's antiscientific emphasis is rooted partly in his personal dislike of most of the technological advances that occurred after his childhood.

Recalling perhaps the great battles between faith and science in the nineteenth and early twentieth centuries, Haldane and others have assumed that Lewis, as one of this century's most well-known advocates of Christianity, felt a natural antipathy for science because of his religious convictions. But this assumption is wide of the mark. First of all, Lewis was aware that many Christians were also scientists (*WLN* 18). Second, Lewis's negative comments about the sciences predate his adult conversion by many years. When he was only seventeen and studying at Great Bookham, Lewis was described by Kirkpatrick as one who "has read . . . more classics than any I ever heard of, unless it be an Addison, Landor, or Macauley," but also one who "knows nothing of science and loathes it and all its works."[8] In 1924—five years before his reconversion to Christianity—Lewis read Haldane's *Daedalus* and pronounced it "a diabolical little book," which should be "read and digested—or vomited" (*DCSL* 287).

The real opposition for Lewis was not science vs. faith but rather science vs. the humanities. In *English Literature in the Sixteenth Century, Excluding Drama,* Lewis offers a summary of Western culture that places the sciences at a point twice removed from the ancient authorities: "Perhaps every new learning makes room for itself by creating a new ignorance. In our own age we have seen the sciences beating back the humanities as humanism once beat back metaphysics. Man's power of attention seems limited; one nail drives out another" (31). Lewis's attitude here is not at all atypical. His contemporary C. P. Snow coined the term "the two cultures" to describe what he called the "gulf of mutual incomprehension" between "literary intellectuals" and scientists. Snow offers a variety of examples to illustrate how bipolar the intellectual life of England and America had become in the fifties (and still is?), but most of his general discussion of the misunderstanding, even hostility, between the two camps applies with special relevance to the controversies between Lewis and Haldane.[9]

Lewis's antagonism to science, however, has often been overstated. Philip Deasy, for example, called the trilogy "a total and unrelenting attack on science."[10] Bruce R. Reichenbach offers a more measured and careful critique, noting that Lewis's chief concerns were the reduction of everything, even values, to the mathematical and the mechanical; the rapid development of technology without regard for long-term effects; the idea of "progress" as automatic and morally imperative; the banality of mass culture; and the brutality of much scientific research on animals.[11] All in all, Reichenbach's is the most sensible and balanced study of Lewis's attitudes toward science and technology and one that shows Lewis's opinions to be prescient more often than they were simply crotchety. Indeed, Lewis's concerns about exploitation of the environment for short-term economic goals and about the needless suffering of animals used in scientific research anticipate widespread public awareness of these issues by almost a half-century.

Another major question for critics has been whether or not Lewis's attitudes toward women in the trilogy are sexist or even misogynist. Doris Myers complains of the "patronizing masculine superiority of Lewis,"[12] and *The Encyclopedia of Science Fiction* calls his views of womanhood "deeply conservative, and also sexist."[13] Margaret Hannay goes a step further in her article "C. S. Lewis: Mere Misogyny?" She argues that all of Lewis's books written before his fifties, when he met and married Joy Davidman, are misogynist. She contends that the Green Lady "degenerates into a simpering fool" at the end of *Perelandra* and that Jane Studdock in *That Hideous Strength* is "ridiculed for her attempted scholarship and berated for not having conceived a child" in *That Hideous Strength.*[14]

Surveying the trilogy, it is not difficult to find passages that lead to charges of sexism. In *Out of the Silent Planet* a pfifltrigg tells Ransom that "the sorns make least account of females and we make most" (116). This implies that women are somewhat out of their element among that world's thinkers and most at home among males who work with their hands. The phrasing also suggests that males define the character of each species, while the females serve as adjuncts to the males.

In *Perelandra* the problem passages occur near the end of the story, where the king is appointed to rule the queen, who submits as part of her proper station. However, it is not clear how the Green Lady is reduced to "a simpering fool" in *Perelandra.* Tinidril's joy at coreigning with the king is never treated by Lewis as simpering, and her submission to his authority is not at all foolish in a hierarchical world. In his depiction of Adam's headship, Lewis closely follows Milton, who has Eve tell Adam,

> My Author and Disposer, what thou bidd'st
> Unargu'd I obey; so God ordains,
> God is thy law, thou mine. (4, 635–37)

Lewis observed in *A Preface to Paradise Lost* that, according to Milton, Adam's great fault in Milton's epic was uxoriousness, obeying his subordinate rather than ruling her (68).

If anything, one would expect charges of sexism to come from Lewis's portrayal of the Green Lady not as too degraded but as too exalted. Lewis's depiction of unfallen womanhood in *Perelandra* is so idealized that it seems irrelevant to the roles of actual women on earth. Male writers are often guilty of an Ave/Eva complex, in which the only women characters they present are sentimentalized madonnas or voluptuous temptresses. Lewis in fact commented in a letter that he was trying to capture both Eve and the Madonna in the Green Lady for the purposes of his theme (*LCSL* 195), so his portrait of her cannot be dismissed as unconscious male chauvinism.

Charges of sexism usually focus most directly on *That Hideous Strength.* There Jane Studdock is presented as "not perhaps a very original thinker," doing her doctoral thesis on Donne's "triumphant vindication of the body" (14). The satirical elements here are multiple, and they are not all directed at Jane's mistaken sense of her femininity. Lewis did not like the idea of doctoral theses. He thought it was clear that those with fellowships at a college would engage in publishable research, and that having an extra degree to certify research skills was redundant and perhaps too American. Second, Lewis believed Donne was as overrated in the twentieth century as he had been underrated in the eighteenth century (*SLE* 106). Lewis's massive volume of the *Oxford History of English Literature* devotes only five pages to a discussion of Donne. So for Jane to be working on Donne suggests that she too has been caught up in the whirligig of modernist fashion. But these are gibes at the state of contemporary academia in general, not specific disparagements of Jane as a female.

Charges of sexism may be more cogently founded upon the narrator's comment that Jane was not a very original thinker and that she had postponed having children so that she could complete her doctoral work. Lewis felt that the cult of originality was another modern aberration, so what seems like a slighting reference here may actually be a backhanded compliment. But the reference to postponing children definitely implies that her first role is as a mother, not as a scholar. This assumption becomes clearer later on, when Merlin thinks Jane ought to be beheaded because the Studdocks' use of contraception has prevented the next pendragon from being born at the appointed hour (278). And at the end of *That*

Hideous Strength, Ransom dismisses Jane with this benediction: "You will have no more dreams. Have children instead" (380).

If Jane is intended by Lewis as the model for all women, then Lewis's views are certainly sexist. It would be highly presumptuous of Lewis to produce simple answers of right and wrong to complex issues of contraception, and of the right—or need—for married women to work outside the home. But it is not clear that Lewis intends Jane to be normative for all women. Two of the other positive St. Anne's characters in the story are Grace Ironwood, an unmarried, professional woman (a physician), and Mother Dimble, who is not able to have children of her own. Neither of these two is portrayed patronizingly or satirically. Also, Jane's desire to be taken more seriously as a scholar is not presented as a peculiarly female trait in *That Hideous Strength.* The same is even more true of her husband, Mark, and of his boorish associate, Curry.

The other controversial passage in *That Hideous Strength* relating to charges of sexism is the one where Ransom explains to Jane the need for wives to obey their husbands. Jane assumes that love requires equality, but Ransom retorts that "equality is not the deepest thing"; equal rights must be guarded by the law because humans are fallen, but equality "guards life; it doesn't make it. It is medicine, not food" (148).

We know that Ransom is speaking for Lewis here, because Lewis makes the same arguments, using identical phrasing, in his essay "Membership," published the same year as *That Hideous Strength.* Lewis's comments on marital roles contribute to a dialogue that has been going on for centuries. In the Christian church, going back at least as far as Chaucer, there has been ongoing dispute about the roles of women and men in marriage. The traditionalists invoke a hierarchical model and quote the apostle Paul on the headship of husbands (Eph. 5:23) and on the need for male authority in the church (1 Tim. 2:12). The egalitarians quote the apostle Paul in saying, "In Christ, there is no male and female" (Gal. 3:28), and note that the early church granted women positions of significant leadership before it began to imitate the polity of the Roman Empire.

Lewis's views about marriage are less a matter of personal eccentricity or hatred of women than of his aligning himself, as he usually did, with the more traditionalist elements of the church. Though he proclaimed himself a democrat because of the need to spread out power after the Fall, he believed that some sense of hierarchy was still required in marriage.

Perhaps it would have been wiser for an unmarried person to speak more tentatively on this topic. When Lewis wed Joy Davidman more than a decade after writing *That Hideous Strength,* he married a very strong personality and did not seem to invoke his hierarchical authority very often, if at all. It also seems somewhat presumptuous of Lewis to have Ransom say that he learned his traditionalist views from the eldils, those who are not "old fashioned; but they are very, very old" (*THS* 146). Here Lewis takes a complex and perennial debate and declares his views are literally on the side of the angels. It is rather like having someone write a story in which the archangel Gabriel comes to earth and advises everyone to vote Republican.

Lewis's views, however, are not predictably chauvinistic. He shows the men and women at St. Anne's sharing household duties, and at the night of the banquet at St. Anne's, the men prepare the food for the women. Lewis also identifies more strongly with Jane's consciousness than with any of the male characters in the story. However much they object to Lewis's views on marriage, women readers of *That Hideous Strength* often identify with Jane's sense that men do not realize how much a woman gives up in marriage (72) or with her resentment of Mark's insensitive and unempathic male nature (315–16).[15]

Owen Barfield concluded that C. S. Lewis was a misogynist on the theoretical level but was not so in his relationships with individual women.[16] Like much of what Barfield said about his friend of nearly forty years, this remark seems curiously ungenerous. But it does reflect a fairly widespread and fairly well-supported perception of Lewis. For one can find a number of slighting references to women, sometimes probably unconscious, in his books and letters. In *Surprised by Joy* Lewis declares Barfield himself to be "as fascinating (and infuriating) as a woman" (200), implying that all women share certain generic traits. In a diary entry written in 1922, Lewis noted that at the school of English at Oxford "women, Indians, and Americans predominate and—I can't say how—one feels a certain amateurishness in the talk and the look of the people" (*DCSL* 120). One suspects that their air of amateurishness may have come from the very fact that they were women, Indians, and Americans. And in *That Hideous Strength* the narrator twice describes the company at St. Anne's by specifying or enumerating the males present, and then lumping the females together as "the women" (292, 320).

Paradoxically, in the published personal reminiscences about Lewis, the women contributors unfailingly describe him in positive terms, while the men offer mixed responses. Patricia (Boshell) Heidelberger, who stayed at the Kilns during the early years of World War II, recalls that Lewis voluntarily coached her in Latin and Greek in order to prepare her for studies at Oxford and that he made a secret arrangement with her mother to pay her tuition.[17] Jill (Flewett) Freud, who stayed at the Kilns later in the war, remembers that Lewis lent her books and even allowed her to charge books on his account at Blackwells bookstore. She says that Lewis built up her self-esteem and taught her to believe in herself as an intelligent human being.[18] Lewis also paid for her to have professional acting lessons. Rosamund Cowan, one of Lewis's first women pupils, said that she was intimidated at first because of his reputation as a "man's man," but she found him courteous, stimulating, intellectually demanding—in sum, "a joy to study with."[19] These and other reminiscences by women who knew Lewis reinforce the idea that Jane Studdock is not intended to show that women have no place in academia or in the professional world. If Lewis did feel patronizing toward women, his attitude in person manifested itself primarily in the form of sensitivity, courtesy, generosity, and respect. Simply to dismiss Lewis as sexist does not do justice to the complexity of his attitudes or behavior toward women.

An equally complex question is Lewis's use of violence in the trilogy, which increases with each successive book. In *Out of the Silent Planet* the violence is mild, and so the response from critics has been mild. There the buffoon-villain Weston, who is responsible for the death of Hyoi the hross, is punished by nothing more severe than having his head dunked in cold water (130). Though W. W. Robson criticizes the "undergraduate humor" of Weston's humiliation,[20] few can take offense at such a punishment. However, in *Perelandra* Weston is physically destroyed, a fate that made critics far more uncomfortable. As discussed in chapters 2 and 5, any attempt to understand the resolution of conflict in *Perelandra* must take into account the mythic element of the narrative, as well as its psychological symbolism.

The ending of *That Hideous Strength* has elicited the greatest concern by far about Lewis's use of violence. One reviewer complained that the victory of Ransom and Merlin was achieved "by brutal, quite unethical, force, by, in fact, mass murder."[21] Another called this "one of the most savage scenes in modern literature."[22] Yet a third objects to the "excessive horror" of the closing pages of *That Hideous Strength*.[23]

Perhaps the first thing to keep in mind in this context is that Lewis was writing during the bleakest years of World War II and that he draws explicit parallels between the leaders of N.I.C.E. and the Nazis: their secret police is more powerful than civil authorities; they control the press; they use criminals for barbaric medical experiments; they dream of creating a master race. Mark learns that his superiors at N.I.C.E. are involved in a conspiracy that engineered both world wars and is planning fourteen more (*THS* 259). So the destruction of N.I.C.E. for the first readers of *That Hideous Strength* would be the fictionalized equivalent of having Hitler and his henchman destroyed by a well-placed bomb.

But critics point out that Lewis does not just summarily execute everyone at N.I.C.E.; he describes their deaths in gruesome detail. Part of the reason for this is probably to sustain the Dantean atmosphere in the scenes at N.I.C.E. Without a doubt *The Inferno* is a lot more gruesome than *That Hideous Strength.*

The difficulty that some readers encounter here, as in *Perelandra,* seems to be rooted in genre expectation. In a fairy tale, the witch who threatens Hansel and Gretel is herself thrown into the oven.

The narrative does not pause to describe her suffering. In chivalric romances, when a fortress of infidels is overthrown, no one stops to inquire about humane conditions for the prisoners. Lewis calls his stories "romances" and "fairy tales," implying that the same emotional boundaries should be applied to his own fiction. Unfortunately, many of his readers are not able to comply. The fault here, I think, is in Lewis more than in his readers. The genres Lewis invokes—romance, fairy tale, tall story—are not crowded with ideas and realistic details the way *That Hideous Strength* is. The first two-thirds of the novel are written as contemporary satire on fashionable ideas, so that readers expect the antagonists to be refuted, converted, out-quipped or silenced—but not slain. Like *Perelandra,* the transition from novel of ideas to myth happens too quickly.

As is so often true, the most penetrating critic of Lewis's narrative strategy is Lewis himself, as expressed in a critique of George Macdonald he wrote seven years before the trilogy.

> I wonder did he indulge (day-dreamily) an otherwise repressed fund of indignation by putting up in his novels bogeys to whom his heroes could make stunning retorts and deliver the stunning blows which he himself neither could nor would deliver in real life. I am certain that this is morally as well as artistically dangerous and I'll tell you why. The *pleasure* of anger—the gnawing attraction which makes one return again and again to its theme—lies, I believe, in the fact that one feels entirely righteous oneself only when one is angry. *Then* the other person is pure black, and you are pure white. But in real life sanity always returns to break the dream. In fiction you can put absolutely *all* the right, with no snags or reservations, on the side of the hero (with whom you identify yourself) and all the wrong on the side of the villain. You thus revel in unearned self-righteousness, which would be vicious even if it were earned. (*TST* 403)

As Lewis's own comments from an earlier year suggest, his art would have been strengthened if he had sought to convey more fully the emotional complexity of actual life, rather than creating villains incapable of moral growth and suitable only for destruction.

In focusing on controversial aspects of the trilogy, however, there is a danger of implying that the Ransom books make for highly problematic reading. But *Out of the Silent Planet, Perelandra,* and

That Hideous Strength continue to be best-sellers a half-century after they were written. And they have received more critical attention in the last decade than in any decade since they were published. A balanced assessment of the trilogy must also try to specify some of its excellences.

The first is the sense of actuality Lewis creates, making the imaginary and exotic seem palpable and tangible. The reader can sense with Ransom first panoramas, new creatures, the weather of other worlds, their dangers, and their wonders. As Robert Plank has commented, "Lewis puts his imagined Mars and Venus before us so vividly, in such corporeal reality, that we not only believe (while we read) such improbable worlds to exist, but also get immersed in them to the extent that we see, feel, and smell them. All writers of heterotopias . . . have attempted this, but few have so gloriously succeeded."[24]

The second excellence, related to the first, is Lewis's evocative prose. Even writers with fertile imaginations may not have the verbal skill to do justice to their visions. But in *Out of the Silent Planet* Lewis captivates readers with his prose tableaus of space, of the Malacandrian landscape, of eldils, of Meldilorn, of watching the planet Jupiter rise over Mars. In *Perelandra* as well there are numerous passages more distinguished than anything that Lewis produced as a poet: Ransom's arrival upon Perelandra, his experience of the bubble-tree and the gourd, his first full vision of an unfallen lady, and the Great Dance. Victor Hamm praised the prose style of *Perelandra* for its "élan and lucidity, and the Shelleyan buoyancy."[25]

A third excellence is Lewis's intellectual energy and broad synthesis of ideas in the trilogy. Though the exposition sometimes looms too large, Lewis generally packs an amazing amount of history, theology, psychology, and cultural criticism into a readable narrative. A. N. Wilson's remarks about *Out of the Silent Planet* are true of the trilogy as a whole: "The author is firing on all cylinders. It brings together Lewis the scholar, Lewis the voracious reader of anything from medieval schoolmen or Italian epic to modern science fiction, Lewis the Christian apologist, Lewis the satirist in the savage tradition of Swift, Lewis the poet."[26]

Fourth, Lewis has embued his fiction with a rare mythic quality. In *Voyages to the Moon,* Marjorie Hope Nicholson describes her response when she began reading the trilogy: "*Out of the Silent Planet* is to me the most beautiful of all cosmic voyages and in some ways the most moving. . . . Earlier writers have created new worlds from legend, from mythology, from fairy tale. Mr. Lewis has created *myth* itself, myth woven of desires and aspirations deep-seated in some, at least of the human race. . . . As I journey with him into worlds at once familiar and strange, I experience, as did Ransom, 'a sensation not of following an adventure but of enacting a myth.' "[27] Chad Walsh offers a similar tribute to the second book of the trilogy: "*Perelandra* is, in sum, an astonishing achievement, and of a high mythic order. By an act of imagination, both probing and soaring, Lewis has created a world in which goodness is at least as convincing as evil. . . . To read the book and then return in thought and activity to this planet is to see the familiar world in a very unfamiliar light."[28] The concluding book of the trilogy is commended for the same qualities by Nathan Comfort Starr, in *King Arthur Today:* "*That Hideous Strength* deserves an honored place in the Arthurian legend, for it is a highly original restatement of old truths applied to our violent, distraught world, and it is conceived in terms of vaulting imagination."[29]

Though Lewis is often credited with mythopoesis, (or myth making), it might be more accurate to describe him as a "re-mythologizer," one who takes old myths that have been largely discarded in the modern world and revitalizes them with his unique blend of intellectual and imaginative ingenuity. Over against contemporary notions of a vast, empty universe where life on earth is but a cosmic fluke, Lewis reintroduces the possibility of a Benevolence at the center of things, of hidden order in what looks like chaos, and of unseen realities that help make sense of that which is seen.

Perhaps the most memorable quality of the trilogy is the author's vision. Lewis's worldview rested upon a complex foundation of philosophy, theology, cultural history, and personal experiences. But larger than all these is a consistent vision into which Lewis could pour all his ideas, feelings, and convictions. According to the old proverb, "Without a vision, the people perish." Lewis came into the world without such a vision. But he found one. And through his powers of intellect, imagination, and utterance, he regales his readers with that vision and invites them to share in it.

APPENDIX

"The Dark Tower"

ACCORDING TO Walter Hooper, who was Lewis's personal secretary for part of the summer of 1963, Lewis left behind after his death an incomplete sixty-four-page manuscript that Hooper named "The Dark Tower." Apparently begun as the sequel to *Out of the Silent Planet,* Lewis abandoned the story after about thirty-two thousand words—either because he had written himself into a corner or because he set it aside in favor of other projects and never returned to it. Whereas *Out of the Silent Planet* presents another world that comes close to Lewis's idea of utopia, "The Dark Tower" presents another world that is clearly a dystopia. In a number of ways, "The Dark Tower" anticipates the scenes depicting N.I.C.E. in *That Hideous Strength.*

The closing words of *Out of the Silent Planet* prepare the way for a sequel. Lewis ends by quoting Ransom as saying, "If there is to be any more space-travelling, it will have to be time-travelling as well . . . !" (160). This hint is picked up by the opening lines of "The Dark Tower": " 'Of course,' said Orfieu, 'the sort of time-travelling you read about in books—time-travelling in the body—is absolutely impossible' " (*DT* 17). Orfieu, a scientist at Cambridge, is explaining to a group of dons he has invited to his rooms that one cannot literally travel in time because the molecules of one's body would still be in existence in the other time but would be disseminated into other material things. His audience includes his assistant, Scudamour, as well as Ransom, Lewis, and the skeptical Scotsman MacPhee.

After an overly protracted discussion about the nature of time and consciousness, Orfieu and his assistant demonstrate a device for seeing other times, which Ransom dubs a chronoscope. On a screen they view some other world dominated by a dark tower in a place and time that they do not recognize. That evening the group gathers for a second session with the chronoscope, and they view a hellish scenario: in a dark room crowded with grotesque ornamentation, there sits an idol, with many bodies all connected to one giant head, and a man—sallow, preternaturally dark-haired, and with a horn, or stinger, in his forehead. When a young man in ritual garb enters and prays to the idol, the horned man stings him in the spine. The young man writhes in pain for a few moments, then regains control, but leaves the room with jerky, robotic movements. The viewers see this repulsive scene reiterated three more times, with the victims changed from humans to automatons, as the Stingingman, "with neither cruelty nor pity," stings each one "with the passionless precision of an insect or a machine" (35).

At future viewings of "Othertime," the dons recognize the dark tower as a replica of the university library at Cambridge. They also see a young man on the screen who is the double of Orfieu's assistant Scudamour. This is disconcerting enough, but later they watch Scudamour's double undergo a painful metamorphosis and grow a stinger in his forehead. Worse yet, a double of Scudamour's fiancée Camilla appears in the idol room, apparently the next victim of the Scudamour-turned-Stingingman. This is too much for Scudamour to take, and he rushes at the chronoscope, smashing it to pieces. His rash action causes the two Scudamours to change worlds: Scudamour finds himself in the idol room with the other Camilla and with a stinger in his forehead. The other Scudamour appears in Orfieu's rooms and quickly makes his escape.

In Othertime, Scudamour tries to reassure Camilla that he is not going to sting her, but she explains she will be thrown into a fire if she does not undergo the stinging ritual. He soon learns that, as the Stingingman, he is the lord of Othertime and that the city of the dark tower is being besieged by White Riders, invaders who seek to destroy the Stingingman and the automatons he has brought into being. He goes into a library and reads an excessively technical discussion about how different time frames can exist in separate dimensions, with the suggestion that the scientists of Othertime have exchanged people from their world with their counterparts in our world. At this point the manuscript breaks off.

Even though "The Dark Tower" is only about seventy-five printed pages, it does reveal the mind, and narrative skill, of Lewis. The depiction of the idol room and the Stingingman vividly evokes an atmosphere of nightmare; one suspects it is based on one of Lewis's own nightmares. According to Hooper, some of the Inklings thought that the stinging episodes had disquieting sexual overtones, and this may be one reason Lewis abandoned the project (*DT* 96). But he does manage to present some deft satire in the pages he completed. First, there is Knellie, an addle-brained "progressive" who calls Lewis "Lu-Lu" and who watches the chronoscope thinking it is some sort of performance art. Then there is Camilla, Scudamour's outspoken fiancée: "She was so free to talk about things her grandmother could not mention that Ransom once said he wondered if she were free to talk about anything else" (76).

"The Dark Tower" hints at some of the themes that are developed in the other Ransom fantasies. The idol with its many bodies and one head probably represents Lewis's distaste for collectivism. The sting that turns people into automatons similarly suggests dehumanization. Othertime is also a spiritually barren realm where Scudamour cannot think or say the word *God* because the word does not exist in the language of that dimension. The idea that most strikingly recalls the Ransom trilogy comes when Scudamour browses through a library in the other world and reads of "the theory that certain fabulous creatures, and other images which constantly appeared in the myths of widely separated peoples and in dreams, might be glimpses of realities which exist in a time closely adjacent to our own" (88).

"The Dark Tower" most directly adumbrates *That Hideous Strength.* The Stingingman closely resembles Alcasan, the prisoner whose decapitation provides the head at N.I.C.E. Both have foreign-looking faces, with beards and yellowish skin. The Stingingman is also described as having an expressionless face, as if he were the sudden victim of a guillotine (32), a fate like Alcasan's. MacPhee, whose obstinate skepticism in "The Dark Tower" comes near to stupidity, reappears as a more credible character, a member of Ransom's company at St. Anne's. Of course, the name Camilla reappears in *That Hideous Strength,* though the Camilla of "The Dark Tower" seems more like Jane Studdock early in the novel than like Camilla Denniston. The idea of parallel time frames is put to good use in *That Hideous Strength,* where Merlin lies in a "parachronic state" (226). (Lewis uses this motif even more extensively in the Narnia chronicles.) Lastly, the idol room with its hideous decorations, including a picture of beetles marching in battalions, resembles the wall hangings in the Objective Room at N.I.C.E., which also features a picture crowded with beetles.

Ransom does not have the richness of character in "The Dark Tower" that we find in *Out of the Silent Planet* and *Perelandra.* Orfieu and Scudamour, however, both scientists and non-Christians, are portrayed with more sympathy and complexity than their counterparts in the trilogy.

One can only guess why Lewis never completed "The Dark Tower." He may have felt that the story was overloaded with exposition. The beginning and the end of the fragment make rather dry reading, as Lewis takes pains to try to convince the reader of the scientific plausibility of his story. Perhaps he learned a lesson here: when he did successfully create a sequel to *Out of the Silent Planet,* he dispensed with scientific explanations altogether and just had the Oyarsa deliver Ransom to Perelandra in a casket.

Another possible reason Lewis might have abandoned "The Dark Tower" is that his vision of horror was not counterpoised by any vision of goodness. In the completed stories of the trilogy, there is a balance: the repugnance of the Un-man is offset by the glory of the Green Lady and her world; the odious characters at N.I.C.E. are juxtaposed to the wholesome and winsome world of St. Anne's. But in "The Dark Tower" the Stingingman is by far the most powerful image, and there is nothing beatific about Ransom or his colleagues to counterbalance this miserific vision.

Despite its incompleteness and evident flaws, the "The Dark Tower" remains an intriguing piece of work. It perhaps was a means for Lewis to discover more clearly what he was trying to accomplish in the succeeding books of the trilogy.

NOTES

Introduction

1. George Sayer, *Jack: C. S. Lewis and His Times* (San Francisco: Harper and Row, 1988) 168; James T. Como, ed., "*C. S. Lewis at the Breakfast Table" and Other Reminiscences* (New York: Macmillan, 1979) xxi.

2. Sayer 218.

3. Jocelyn Gibb, ed., *Light on C. S. Lewis* (New York: Harcourt, Brace and World, 1965) 71.

4. Roger Lancelyn Green and Walter Hooper, *C. S. Lewis: A Biography* (New York: Harcourt Brace Jovanovich, 1974) 33.

5. Green and Hooper 160.

6. Como xxi.

7. Helen Gardner, "Clive Staples Lewis, 1898–1963," *Proceedings of the British Academy* 51 (1965): 424.

8. Carolyn Keefe, ed., *C. S. Lewis: Speaker and Teacher* (Grand Rapids, MI: Zondervan, 1971) 105.

9. Paul F. Ford, *Companion to Narnia* (San Francisco: Harper and Row, 1980); Walter Hooper, *Past Watchful Dragons: The Narnian Chronicles of C. S. Lewis* (New York: Collier Books, 1979); Paul Karkainan, *Narnia Explored* (Old Tappan, NJ: Revell, 1979); Kathryn Lindskoog, *The Lion of Judah in Never-Never Land: The Theology of C. S. Lewis Expressed in His Fantasies for Children* (Grand Rapids, MI: Eerdmans, 1973); Peter J. Schakel, *Reading with the Heart: The Way into Narnia* (Grand Rapids, MI: Eerdmans, 1979); Peter J. Schakel, *Reason and Imagination in C. S. Lewis: A Study of Till We Have Faces* (Grand Rapids, MI: Eerdmans, 1984).

10. Macmillan Publishing Company, letter to the author, 9 July 1990.

1. "Transfiguring the Past": Lewis's Reading of His Early Life

1. John Beversluis, *C. S. Lewis and the Search for Rational Religion* (Grand Rapids, MI: Eerdmans, 1985) 9.

2. Brian Murphy, *C. S. Lewis* (Mercer Island, WA: Starmont House, 1983) 17.

3. Qtd. in Sayer 170.

4. Qtd. in Donald E. Glover, *C. S. Lewis and the Art of Enchantment* (Athens: Ohio UP, 1981) 34.

5. Clyde S. Kilby and Marjorie Lamp Mead, eds., *Brothers and Friends: The Diaries of Major Warren Hamilton Lewis* (San Francisco: Harper and Row, 1982) 247; Sayer 25.

6. Green and Hooper 28.

7. Margaret Patterson Hannay, *C. S. Lewis* (New York: Frederick Ungar, 1981) 6.

8. Sayer 45–46.

9. Green and Hooper 43; Sayer 47.

10. Paul F. Ford finds similar connotations to the word *grown-up* throughout the *Chronicles of Narnia.* See Ford 1–2.

11. Sayer 139.

12. Martha C. Sammons, *A Guide through the Ransom Trilogy* (Westchester, IL: Cornerstone Books, 1980) 158, 160.

13. Como xxvii.

2. "Smuggled Theology": The Christian Vision of the Trilogy

1. Glover 38.

2. Humphrey Carpenter, ed., *The Letters of J. R. R. Tolkien* (Boston: Houghton Mifflin, 1981) 29.

3. Carpenter 32–34.

4. John S. Kennedy, "Fiction in Focus," *Sign* 23 (Nov. 1943): 255.

5. Frank Swinnerton, "Our Planet and Others," *Observer* 27 (Nov. 1938): 6.

6. Green and Hooper 163.

7. Olaf Stapledon, *Last and First Men* (Los Angeles: Jeremy P. Tarcher, 1988) 302.

8. Qtd. in *The Penguin Dictionary of Modern Quotations,* ed. J. M. Cohen and M. J. Cohen (New York: Penguin, 1980) 290.

9. Charles Moorman, *The Precincts of Felicity: The Augustinian City of the Oxford Christians* (Gainesville: University of Florida Press, 1966) 109.

10. Glover 79.

11. W. D. Norwood, Jr., "The Neo-Medieval Novels of C. S. Lewis," diss., University of Texas at Austin, 1965, 36.

12. Joe R. Christopher, *C. S. Lewis* (Boston: Twayne, 1987) 93.

13. Evan K. Gibson, *C. S. Lewis: Spinner of Tales: A Guide to His Fiction* (Washington, D.C.: Christian UP, 1980) 40.

14. Carpenter 34.

15. Victor M. Hamm, "Mr. Lewis in Perelandra," *Thought* 20 (June 1945): 271.

16. Glover 30, 37.

17. Ed Chapman, "Toward a Sacramental Ecology: Technology, Nature, and Transcendence in C. S. Lewis's Ransom Trilogy," *Mythlore* 3, no. 4 (n.d.): 14.

18. Gibson 55.

19. Carpenter 29, 378.

20. Qtd. in Glover 76.

21. See Richard Purtill, "*That Hideous Strength:* A Double Story," in *The Longing for a Form: Essays on the Fiction of C. S. Lewis*, ed. Peter J. Schakel (Kent, OH: Kent State UP, 1977) 91–98; Hannay 103; Gibson 72–73.

22. See Green and Hooper 165; J. B. S. Haldane, "Auld Hornie, F. R. S.," *Modern Quarterly* 1 (Autumn 1946): 32–40; rpt. in *Shadows of the Imagination*, ed. Mark R. Hillegas (Carbondale: Southern Illinois UP, 1969) 17–18.

3. The Recovered Image: Elements of Classicism and Medievalism

1. Gibb 61.

2. Kath Filmer, "The Polemic Image: The Role of Metaphor and Symbol in the Fiction of C. S. Lewis," *Seven: An Anglo-American Literary Review* 7 (1986): 64.

3. Norwood 35; Angele Botros Samaan, "C. S. Lewis: The Utopianist and His Critics," *Cairo Studies in English* 1966: 137–38.

4. Gibb 92; Nancy-Lou Patterson, "Anti-Babels: The Images of the Divine Centre in *That Hideous Strength*," in *Mythcon II Proceedings*, ed. Glen Good-Knight (Los Angeles: Mythopoeic Society, 1972) 11.

5. Roland M. Kawano, "C. S. Lewis and the Great Dance," *Christianity and Literature* 26 (Fall 1976): 24.

6. Chad Walsh, *The Literary Legacy of C. S. Lewis* (New York: Harcourt Brace Jovanovich, 1979) 119.

7. Como 111.

8. *The Oxford Companion to the Literature of Wales*, comp. Meic Stephens (Oxford: Oxford UP, 1986) 671.

9. Patterson 8.

4. "Souls Who Have Lost the Intellectual Good": Portraits of Evil

1. Green and Hooper 174.

2. Sayer 63.

5. Ransom and Lewis: Cosmic Voyage as Spiritual Pilgrimage

1. Sayer 153.

2. A. N. Wilson, *C. S. Lewis: A Biography* (New York: W. W. Norton, 1990) 221.

3. Como 54; Douglas H. Gresham, *Lenten Lands* (New York: Macmillan, 1988) 55.

4. Como 53, 71, 93.

5. Glover 77.

6. Walsh 86.

7. Green and Hooper 179.

8. See also Sayer 143.

9. Sayer 206.

10. Como 108; Clare Godfrey, "New Fiction," *New York Herald Tribune Weekly Book Review* 2 Apr. 1944: sec. 6, p. 8.

11. See, for example, Corbin Scott Carnell, "Ransom in C. S. Lewis' *Perelandra* as Hero in Transformation: Notes toward a Jungian Reading of the Novel," *Studies in the Literary Imagination* 14, no. 2 (Fall 1981): 67–71; Lee D. Rossi, *The Politics of Fantasy: C. S. Lewis and J. R. R. Tolkien* (Ann Arbor, MI: UMI Research Press, 1984) 39.

12. Gibb 54.

6. Models, Influences, and Echoes

1. Como xxii.

2. Como 47; Stephen Schofield, ed., *In Search of C. S. Lewis* (South Plainfield, NJ: Bridge Publishing, 1983) 6.

3. Green and Hooper 164.

4. Robert E. Boenig, "Lewis's Time Machine and His Trip to the Moon," *Mythlore* 24 (Summer 1980): 6; Mark R. Hillegas, *The Future as Nightmare: H. G. Wells and the Anti-Utopians* (New York: Oxford UP, 1967) 135.

5. Qtd. in E. F. Bleiler, ed., "C. S. Lewis," in *Supernatural Fiction Writers: Fantasy and Horror,* vol. 2 (New York: Scribner's, 1985) 542.

6. Sayer 153.

7. Sayer 153.

8. Qtd. in Bleiler 541.

9. Jeannette Hume Lutton, "The Feast of Reason: *Out of the Silent Planet* as the Book of Hnau," *Mythlore* 47 (Autumn 1986): 39.

10. Glover 77.

11. Carpenter 89.

12. Glover 77.

13. Colin Hardie, "A Colleague's Note on C. S. Lewis," *Inklings—Jahrbuch für*

Literatur und Ästhetik 3 (1985): 177; Sayer 119; William Griffin, *Clive Staples Lewis: A Dramatic Life* (New York: Harper and Row, 1986) 140; Humphrey Carpenter, *The Inklings: C. S. Lewis, J. R. R. Tolkien, Charles Williams, and their Friends* (Boston: Houghton Mifflin, 1979) 198.

14. Kilby and Mead 36.

15. Martin Moynihan, "C. S. Lewis and T. D. Weldon," *Seven: An Anglo-American Literary Review* 5 (1984): 105.

16. Peter J. Schakel, ed., *The Longing for a Form: Essays on the Fiction of C. S. Lewis* (Kent, OH: Kent State UP, 1977) 73.

17. Green and Hooper 170.

18. Glover 77.

19. C. N. Manlove, *Modern Fantasy: Five Studies* (Cambridge: Cambridge UP, 1975) 119.

20. Green and Hooper 174.

21. Carpenter, *Inklings* 85, 94.

22. Wilson 148.

23. Carpenter, *Letters* 224.

24. Carpenter, *Letters* 361.

25. Sayer 48.

26. Qtd. in Green and Hooper 179.

27. Gibb 49.

28. Wilson 71.

29. Green and Hooper 67, 176.

30. Hillegas 138.

31. Green and Hooper 163–64.

32. Christopher 104.

33. Green and Hooper 174.

7. The Achievement of C. S. Lewis: Assessing the Trilogy

1. Mark R. Hillegas, "Science Fiction and the Idea of Progress," *Extrapolation* 1 (May 1960): 27.

2. Como 74.

3. Haldane 25.

4. Christopher 89–90.

5. Sayer 90.

6. Sayer 168.

7. Sayer 206.

8. Qtd. in Sayer 61–62.

9. C. P. Snow, *The Two Cultures* (Cambridge: Cambridge UP, 1964) 4–7.

10. Philip Deasy, "God, Space, and C. S. Lewis," *Commonweal* 68 (25 July 1958): 422.

11. Bruce R. Reichenbach, "C. S. Lewis on the Desolation of Devalued Science," *Seven: An Anglo-American Literary Review* 4 (1983): 15–18.

12. Doris T. Myers, "Brave New World: The Status of Women according to Tolkien, Lewis, and Williams," *Cimarron Review* 17 (Oct. 1971): 18.

13. Qtd. in John Peters, *C. S. Lewis: The Man and His Achievement* (Exeter, UK: Pater Noster Press, 1985) 27.

14. Margaret Hannay, "C. S. Lewis: Mere Misogyny?" *Daughters of Sarah,* 1 (Sep. 1975): 1, 2.

15. See, for example, Janice Witherspoon Neuleib, "Comic Grotesques: The Means of Revelation in *Wise Blood* and *That Hideous Strength,*" *Christianity and Literature* 30 (Summer 1981): 16; Nancy-Lou Patterson, "Guardaci Ben: The Visionary Woman in C. S. Lewis' Chronicles of Narnia and *That Hideous Strength,*" *Mythlore* 21, no. 4 (Fall 1979): 22.

16. Green and Hooper 213–14.

17. Schofield 54–55.

18. Schofield 57.

19. Schofield 62.

20. W. W. Robson, "C. S. Lewis," *Cambridge Quarterly* 1 (1966): 260.

21. J. D. Beresford, "Five Novels," *Manchester Guardian* 24 Aug. 1945: 3.

22. Qtd. in Nancy-Lou Patterson, "Banquet at Belbury: Festival and Horror in *That Hideous Strength,*" *Mythlore* 29 (Autumn 1981): 7.

23. Edwin Muir, "New Novels," *Listener* 34 (6 Sep. 1945): 274.

24. Mark R. Hillegas, ed., *Shadows of Imagination: The Fantasies of C. S. Lewis, J. R. R. Tolkien, and Charles Williams* (Carbondale: Southern Illinois UP, 1969) 37.

25. Hamm 276.

26. Wilson 154.

27. Qtd. in Green and Hooper 165–66.

28. Walsh 109.

29. Nathan C. Starr, *King Arthur Today: The Arthurian Legend in English and American Literature, 1901–1953* (Gainesville: University of Florida Press, 1954) 187.

BIBLIOGRAPHY

Biographies and Biographical Materials

Barfield, Owen. *Owen Barfield on C. S. Lewis.* Ed. by G. B. Tennyson. Middletown: Wesleyan UP, 1989.

Carpenter, Humphrey. *The Inklings: C. S. Lewis, J. R. R. Tolkien, Charles Williams, and Their Friends.* Boston: Houghton Mifflin, 1979.

——, ed. *The Letters of J. R. R. Tolkien.* Boston: Houghton Mifflin, 1981.

Christopher, Joe R. " 'From the Master's Lips': W. B. Yeats as C. S. Lewis Saw Him." *CSL: The Bulletin of the New York C. S. Lewis Society* 6, i: 14–19.

Como, James T., ed. *"C. S. Lewis at the Breakfast Table" and Other Reminiscences.* New York: Macmillan, 1979.

Dorsett, Lyle W. *And God Came In: The Extraordinary Story of Joy Davidman: Her Life and Marriage to C. S. Lewis.* New York: Macmillan, 1983.

Gardner, Helen. "Clive Staples Lewis, 1898–1963." *Proceedings of the British Academy* 51 (1965): 417–28.

Gibb, Jocelyn, ed. *Light on C. S. Lewis.* New York: Harcourt, Brace and World, 1965.

Gilbert, Douglas, and Clyde S. Kilby. *C. S. Lewis: Images of His World.* Grand Rapids, MI: Eerdmans, 1973.

Green, Roger Lancelyn, and Walter Hooper. *C. S. Lewis: A Biography.* New York: Harcourt Brace Jovanovich, 1974.

Gresham, Douglas H. *Lenten Lands.* New York: Macmillan, 1988.

Griffin, William. *Clive Staples Lewis: A Dramatic Life.* New York: Harper and Row, 1986.

Hardie, Colin. "A Colleague's Note on C. S. Lewis." *Inklings—Jahrbuch für Literatur und Ästhetik* 3 (1985): 177–82.

Hooper, Walter. "Reminiscences." *Mythlore* 12 (June 1976): 5–9.

——. *Through Joy and Beyond: A Pictorial Biography of C. S. Lewis.* New York: Macmillan, 1982.

Keefe, Carolyn, ed. *C. S. Lewis: Speaker and Teacher.* Grand Rapids, MI: Zondervan, 1971.

Kilby, Clyde S., and Marjorie Lamp Mead. *Brothers and Friends: The Diaries of Major Warren Hamilton Lewis.* San Francisco: Harper and Row, 1982.

Moynihan, Martin. "C. S. Lewis and T. D. Weldon." *Seven: An Anglo-American Literary Review* 5 (1984): 101–5.

Sayer, George. *Jack: C. S. Lewis and His Times.* San Francisco: Harper and Row, 1988.

Schofield, Stephen, ed. *In Search of C. S. Lewis.* South Plainfield, NJ: Bridge Publishing, 1983.

Starr, Nathan C. "C. S. Lewis: A Personal Memoir." *Unicorn* 2, no. 2 (Spring 1972): 9–11.

Vanauken, Sheldon. *A Severe Mercy.* New York: Harper and Row, 1977.

Wilson, A. N. *C. S. Lewis: A Biography.* New York: W. W. Norton, 1990.

General Studies of Lewis and His Fiction

Aeschliman, Michael D. *The Restitution of Man: C. S. Lewis and the Case against Scientism.* Grand Rapids, MI: Eerdmans, 1983.

Arnott, Anne. *The Secret Country of C. S. Lewis.* Grand Rapids, MI: Eerdmans, 1975.

Beversluis, John. *C. S. Lewis and the Search for Rational Religion.* Grand Rapids, MI: Eerdmans, 1985.

Campbell, David C., and Dale E. Hess. "Olympian Detachment: A Critical Look at the World of C. S. Lewis's Characters." *Studies in the Literary Imagination* 22 (Fall 1989): 129–48.

Carnell, Corbin Scott. *Bright Shadow of Reality: C. S. Lewis and the Feeling Intellect.* Grand Rapids, MI: Eerdmans, 1974.

Christopher, Joe R. *C. S. Lewis.* Boston: Twayne, 1987.

Cunningham, Richard. *C. S. Lewis: Defender of the Faith.* Philadelphia, Westminster Press, 1967.

Edwards, Bruce L., ed. *The Taste of the Pineapple: Essays on C. S. Lewis as Reader, Critic, and Imaginative Writer.* Bowling Green, OH: Bowling Green State University Popular Press, 1988.

Filmer, Kath. "The Polemic Image: The Role of Metaphor and Symbol in the Fiction of C. S. Lewis." *Seven: An Anglo-American Literary Review* 7 (1986): 61–76.

Fuller, Edmund. *Books with Men behind Them.* New York: Random House, 1962.

Gibson, Evan K. *C. S. Lewis: Spinner of Tales: A Guide to His Fiction.* Washington, D.C.: Christian UP, 1980.

Glover, Donald E. *C. S. Lewis and the Art of Enchantment.* Athens: Ohio UP, 1981.

Green, Roger Lancelyn. *C. S. Lewis.* London: Bodley Head, 1963.

Hannay, Margaret Patterson. *C. S. Lewis.* New York: Frederick Ungar, 1981.

———. "C. S. Lewis: Mere Misogyny?" *Daughters of Sarah* 1 (Sep. 1975): 1–4.

Hart, Dabney Adams. *Through the Open Door: A New Look at C. S. Lewis.* Tuscaloosa: University of Alabama Press, 1984.

Hillegas, Mark R., ed. *Shadows of Imagination: The Fantasies of C. S. Lewis, J. R. R. Tolkien, and Charles Williams.* Carbondale: Southern Illinois UP, 1969.

Holmer, Paul L. *C. S. Lewis: The Shape of His Faith and Thought.* New York: Harper and Row, 1976.

Howard, Thomas. *The Achievement of C. S. Lewis: A Reading of His Fiction.* Wheaton, IL: Harold Shaw Publishers, 1980.

Kilby, Clyde S. *The Christian World of C. S. Lewis.* Grand Rapids, MI: Eerdmans, 1964.

———. *Images of Salvation in the Fiction of C. S. Lewis.* Wheaton, IL: Harold Shaw Publishers, 1978.

Kreeft, Peter. *C. S. Lewis: A Critical Essay.* Grand Rapids, MI: Eerdmans, 1969.

Kuhn, Daniel K. "The Joy of the Absolute: A Comparative Study of the Romantic Visions of William Wordsworth and C. S. Lewis." In *Imagination and the Spirit: Essays in Literature and the Christian Faith Presented to Clyde S. Kilby.* Ed. by Charles Huttar. Grand Rapids, MI: Eerdmans, 1971. Pp. 189–214.

Kuhn, Helmut. "C. S. Lewis: Der Romancier der unerbittlichen Liebe." *Wort und Wahrheit* 10 (Feb. 1955): 113–26.

Lindskoog, Kathryn Ann. *C. S. Lewis: Mere Christian.* Glendale, CA: G/L Publications, 1973.

Manlove, C. W. *C. S. Lewis: His Literary Achievement.* New York: St. Martin's Press, 1987.

Masterman, Margaret. "C. S. Lewis: The Author and the Hero." *Twentieth Century* 158 (Dec. 1955): 539–48.

Meilaender, Gilbert. *The Taste for the Other: The Social and Ethical Thought of C. S. Lewis.* Grand Rapids, MI: Eerdmans, 1978.

Moorman, Charles. *The Precincts of Felicity: The Augustinian City of the Oxford Christians.* Gainesville: University of Florida Press, 1966.

Murphy, Brian. *C. S. Lewis.* Mercer Island, WA: Starmont House, 1983.

———. "Enchanted Romanticism: The Legacy of C. S. Lewis." *Christianity and Literature* 25 (Winter 1976): 13–26.

Norwood, W. D., Jr. "The Neo-Medieval Novels of C. S. Lewis." Diss. University of Texas at Austin, 1965.

Peters, John. *C. S. Lewis: The Man and His Achievement.* Exeter, UK: Pater Noster Press, 1985.

Purtill, Richard. *Lord of Elves and Eldils: Fantasy and Philosophy in C. S. Lewis and J. R. R. Tolkien.* Grand Rapids, MI: Zondervan, 1974.

Reilly, R. J. *Romantic Religion: A Study of Barfield, Lewis, Williams, and Tolkien.* Athens: University of Georgia Press, 1972.

Robson, W. W. "C. S. Lewis." *Cambridge Quarterly* 1 (1966): 252–72.

Rossi, Lee D. *The Politics of Fantasy: C. S. Lewis and J. R. R. Tolkien.* Ann Arbor, MI: UMI Research Press, 1984.

Schakel, Peter J., ed. *The Longing for a Form: Essays on the Fiction of C. S. Lewis.* Kent, OH: Kent State UP, 1977.

——. "The Satiric Imagination of C. S. Lewis." *Studies in the Literary Imagination* 22 (Fall 1989): 129–48.

Smith, Robert Houston. *Patches of Godlight: The Pattern of Thought in C. S. Lewis.* Athens: University of Georgia Press, 1981.

Spivak, Charlotte. "Images of Spirit in the Fiction of C. S. Lewis." *Mythlore* 52 (1987): 32–38.

Stahl, John H. "The Nature and Function of Myth in the Christian Thought of C. S. Lewis." *Christian Scholar's Review* 7 (Fall 1978): 330–36.

Urang, Gunnar. *Shadows of Heaven: Religion and Fantasy in the Writing of C. S. Lewis, Charles Williams, and J. R. R. Tolkien.* Philadelphia: Pilgrim Press, 1971.

Walsh, Chad. *C. S. Lewis: Apostle to the Skeptics.* New York: Macmillan, 1949.

——. "C. S. Lewis: Critic, Creator, and Cult Figure." *Seven: An Anglo-American Literary Review* 2 (1981): 66–80.

——. *The Literary Legacy of C. S. Lewis.* New York: Harcourt Brace Jovanovich, 1979.

Weatherby, H. L. "Two Medievalists: Lewis and Eliot on Christianity and Literature." *Sewanee Review* 78 (Spring 1970): 330–47.

White, Luther William. *The Image of Man in C. S. Lewis.* Nashville: Abingdon Press, 1969.

Willis, John Randolph. *Pleasures Forevermore: The Theology of C. S. Lewis.* Chicago: Loyola UP, 1983.

Wright, Marjorie Evelyn. "The Vision of the Cosmic Order in the Oxford Mythmakers." In *Imagination and the Spirit: Essays in Literature and the Christian Faith Presented to Clyde S. Kilby.* Ed. by Charles Huttar. Grand Rapids, MI: Eerdmans, 1971. Pp. 259–76.

Studies Relating Generally to the Ransom Trilogy

Bailey, James Osler. *Pilgrims through Space and Time: Trends and Patterns in Scientific and Utopian Fiction.* New York: Argus Books, 1947.

Bleiler, E. F., ed. "C. S. Lewis." In *Supernatural Fiction Writers: Fantasy and Horror.* Vol. 2. New York: Scribner's, 1985.

Carnell, Corbin Scott. "The Meaning of Masculine and Feminine in the Work of C. S. Lewis." *Modern British Literature* 2 (1977): 153–59.

Chapman, Ed. "Toward a Sacramental Ecology: Technology, Nature, and Transcendence in C. S. Lewis's Ransom Trilogy." *Mythlore* 3, no. 4 (n.d.): 10–16.

Christopher, J. R. "A Glossary of Old Solar." *Parma Eldalamberon* (Buena Vista, CA) 1, no. 1 (1971): 4–7.

Clute, John. "C. S. Lewis, 1898–1963." In *Science Fiction Writers: Critical Studies of the Major Authors from the Early Nineteenth Century to the Present Day.* Ed. by E. F. Bleiler. New York: Scribner's, 1982. Pp. 243–48.

Dana, Margaret. "The Tao of Space Travel." *Lamp-post* 3 (July–Oct. 1979): 4–8.

Deasy, Philip. "God, Space, and C. S. Lewis." *Commonweal* 68 (25 July 1958): 421–53.

Fuller, Edmund. "The Christian Spaceman: C. S. Lewis." *Horizon* 1 (May 1959): 64–69, 125–27.

Green, Roger Lancelyn. *Into Other Worlds: Space-Flight in Fiction, from Lucian to Lewis.* London: Abelard-Schuman, 1958.

Grennan, Margaret R. "The Lewis Trilogy: A Scholar's Holiday." *Catholic World* 167 (July 1948): 337–44.

Haldane, J. B. S. "Auld Hornie, F. R. S." *Modern Quarterly* 1 (Autumn 1946): 32–40. Rpt. in *Shadows of the Imagination.* Ed. by Mark R. Hillegas. Carbondale: Southern Illinois UP, 1969.

Hillegas, Mark R. *The Future as Nightmare: H. G. Wells and the Anti-Utopians.* New York: Oxford UP, 1967.

———. "Science Fiction and the Idea of Progress." *Extrapolation* 1 (May 1960): 25–28.

Hilton-Young, Wayland. "The Contented Christian." *Cambridge Journal* 5 (July 1952): 603–12.

Howard, Thomas. "The 'Moral Mythology' of C. S. Lewis." *Modern Age* 22 (Fall 1978): 384–92.

Hume, Kathryn. "C. S. Lewis' Trilogy: A Cosmic Romance." *Modern Fiction Studies* 20 (1974): 505–17.

Irwin, W. R. " 'There and Back Again': The Romances of Williams, Lewis, and Tolkien." *Sewanee Review* 69 (1961): 566–78.

Manlove, C. N. *Modern Fantasy: Five Studies.* Cambridge: Cambridge UP, 1975.

McNelly, Willis E. "Science Fiction and Religion." *America* 10 (May 1980): 394–97.

Moorman, Charles. "Space Ship and Grail: The Myths of C. S. Lewis." *College English* 18 (May 1957): 401–5.

Myers, Doris T. "Brave New World: The Status of Women according to Tolkien, Lewis, and Williams." *Cimarron Review* 17 (Oct. 1971): 13–19.

Nardo, A. K. "Decorum in the Fields of Arbol: Interplanetary Genres in C. S. Lewis's Space Trilogy." *Extrapolation* 20 (Summer 1979): 118–28.

Neuleib, Janice Witherspoon. "Of Other Worlds: Worldly Wisdom As It Grows in Science Fiction." *Extrapolation* 19 (May 1978): 108–11.

———. "Technology and Theocracy: The Cosmic Voyages of Wells and Lewis." *Extrapolation* 16 (May 1975): 130–36.

Norwood, W. D., Jr. "C. S. Lewis, Owen Barfield, and Modern Myth." *Midwest Quarterly* 8 (Spring 1967): 279–91.

———. "Unifying Themes in C. S. Lewis' Trilogy." *Critique* 9 (Nov. 1965): 67–80.

Phelan, John M. "Men and Morals in Space." *America* 113 (9 Oct. 1965): 405–07.

Philmus, Robert M. "C. S. Lewis and the Fictions of 'Scientism.'" *Extrapolation* 13 (1972): 92–101.

Plank, Robert. "Some Psychological Aspects of Lewis's Trilogy." In *Shadows of Imagination: The Fantasies of C. S. Lewis, J. R. R. Tolkien, and Charles Williams.* Ed. by Mark R. Hillegas. Carbondale: Southern Illinois UP, 1969. Pp. 26–40.

Purtill, Richard L. "Mind, Matter, and Magic in Fantasy and Science Fiction." In *The Transcendent Adventure: Studies of Religion in Science Fiction/Fantasy.* Ed. by Robert Reilly. Westport, CT: Greenwood Press, 1985. Pp. 27–35.

Redmann, Sister Esther. "From Mere Christian to Alter Christus." *Lamp-post* 3, no. 2 (Apr. 1979): 3–5.

Sale, Roger. "England's Parnassus: C. S. Lewis, Charles Williams, J. R. Tolkien [*sic*]." *Hudson Review* 17 (Summer 1964): 203–25.

Samaan, Angele Botros. "C. S. Lewis: The Utopianist and His Critics." *Cairo Studies in English* 1966: 137–66.

Sammons, Martha C. *A Guide through the Ransom Trilogy.* Westchester, IL: Cornerstone Books, 1980.

Scholes, Robert, and Eric S. Rabkin. *Science Fiction: History, Science, Vision.* New York: Oxford UP, 1977.

Shumaker, Wayne. "The Cosmic Trilogy of C. S. Lewis." *Hudson Review* 8, no. 2 (Summer 1955): 51–63. Rpt. in *The Longing for a Form: Essays on the Fiction of C. S. Lewis.* Ed. by Peter J. Schakel. Kent, OH: Kent State UP, 1977. Pp. 51–63.

Spacks, Patricia Meyer. "The Mythmaker's Dilemma: Three Novels by C. S. Lewis." *Discourse* 2 (Oct. 1959): 234–44.

Timmerman, John H. *Of Other Worlds: The Fantasy Genre.* Bowling Green, OH: Bowling Green UP, 1983.

Walsh, Chad. *From Utopia to Nightmare.* New York: Harper and Row, 1962.

Out of the Silent Planet

REVIEWS

Brady, Charles A. *Best Sellers* 4 (15 May 1944): 40–41.

Keenan, Charles. "One Universe." *America* 70 (23 Oct. 1943): 77–78.

Kennedy, John S. "Fiction in Focus." *Sign* 23 (Nov. 1943): 255.

Lewis, Elaine Lambert. "Fiction." *Library Journal* 68 (1 Sep. 1943): 668.

"Little Hman, What Hnau?" *Time* 42 (11 Oct. 1943): 100, 102, 104.

Mascall, E. L. "Book Reviews." *Theology* 38 (Apr. 1938): 303–4.

Neider, Charles. "Novels: Fact and Fantasy." *New York Herald Tribune* 3 Oct. 1943: sec. 8, pp. 12, 14.

"New Novels." *The Times* 1 Oct. 1938: sec. C, p. 7.

North, Jessica Nelson. "Sorns, Hrossa for the 'Bent.'" *Chicago Sun Book Week* 19 Sep. 1943: sec. 5, p. 9.

Redman, Ben Ray. "C. S. Lewis's Magnificent Fantasy." *Saturday Review of Literature* 26 (16 Oct. 1943): 52.

Reynolds, Horace. "Rocket to Mars." *New York Times Book Review* 3 Oct. 1943: sec. 7, p. 16.

Swinnerton, Frank. "Our Planet and Others." *Observer* 27 (Nov. 1938): 6.

CRITICAL INTERPRETATIONS

Brown, Judith. "The Pilgrimage from Deep Space." *Mythlore* 4, no. 3 (1973): 13–15.

Carleton, Jim. "Wondelone." *Parma Eldalamberon* (Buena Vista, CA) 1, no. 1 (1971): 7–8.

Farley, Karen. "Philology in *Out of the Silent Planet.*" *CSL: The Bulletin of the New York C. S. Lewis Society* 2 (Oct. 1971): 3.

Hannay, Margaret. "The Mythology of *Out of the Silent Planet.*" *Mythlore* 1, no. 4 (1969): 11–14.

Hillegas, Mark R. "Science Fiction as Cultural Phenomenon: A Re-evaluation." *Extrapolation* 4 (May 1963): 26–33.

Hodgens, Richard. "Star-Begotten on the Silent Planet." *CSL: The Bulletin of the New York C. S. Lewis Society* 3 (Feb. 1972): 7.

Hollwitz, John. "The Wonder of Passage, the Making of Gold: Alchemy and Initiation in *Out of the Silent Planet.*" *Mythlore* 11 (Winter–Spring 1985): 17–24.

Lutton, Jeannette Hume. "The Feast of Reason: *Out of the Silent Planet* as the Book of Hnau." *Mythlore* 47 (Autumn 1986): 37–42.

Musacchio, George. "Elwin Ransom: The Pilgrimage Begins." *Mythlore* 50 (Summer 1987): 15–17.

Walsh, Chad. "The Reeducation of a Fearful Pilgrim." In *The Longing for a Form: Essays on the Fiction of C. S. Lewis.* Ed. by Peter J. Schakel. Kent, OH: Kent State UP, 1977. Pp. 64–72.

Perelandra

REVIEWS

Bacon, Leonard. "The Imaginative Power of C. S. Lewis." *Saturday Review of Literature* 27 (8 Apr. 1944): 9.

Brunini, John C. "Books of the Week." *Commonweal* 40 (2 May 1944): 90–91.

Clare, Tullis. "Paradise Unlost." *Time and Tide* 24 (1 May 1943): 362–63.

Cooke, Alistair. "Mr. Anthony at Oxford." *New Republic* 24 Apr. 1944: 578–80.

Donaghy, William A. "Salathiel's Progress: Perelandra." *America* 71 (29 Apr. 1944): 104.

Farber, Marjorie. "Imperfect Paradise." *New York Times Book Review* 26 Mar. 1944: 4.

Godfrey, Clare. "New Fiction." *New York Herald Tribune Weekly Book Review* 2 Apr. 1944: sec. 6, p. 8.

Hamm, Victor M. "Mr. Lewis in Perelandra." *Thought* 20 (June 1945): 271–90.

Hobson, Harold. "A Novel of Adam and Eve on the Planet Venus: A London Letter." *Christian Science Monitor Weekly Magazine Section* 5 June 1943: 11.

Muir, Edwin. "New Novels." *Listener* 29 (6 Mar. 1943): 546.

O'Brien, Kate. "Fiction." *Spectator* 170 (14 May 1943): 458.

Pryce-Jones, Alan. "New Novels." *Observer* 25 Apr. 1943: 3.

CRITICAL INTERPRETATIONS

Burgess, Andrew J. "The Concept of Eden." In *The Transcendent Adventure: Studies of Religion in Science Fiction/Fantasy.* Ed. by Robert Reilly. Westport, CT: Greenwood Press, 1985. Pp. 73–81.

Carnell, Corbin Scott. "Ransom in C. S. Lewis' *Perelandra* as Hero in Transformation: Notes toward a Jungian Reading of the Novel." *Studies in the Literary Imagination* 14, no. 2 (Fall 1981): 67–71.

Como, James. "Myth and Belief in Perelandra." *CSL: The Bulletin of the New York C. S. Lewis Society* 4, no. 2: 2–7.

Gibson, Evan K. "The Centrality of *Perelandra* to Lewis's Theology." In *G. K. Chesterton and C. S. Lewis: The Riddle of Joy.* Ed. by Michael H. Macdonald and Andrew A. Tadie. Grand Rapids, MI: Eerdmans, 1989. Pp. 125–38.

Hannay, Margaret. "The Mythology of *Perelandra.*" *Mythlore* 2 (Winter 1970): 14–16.

———. "A Preface to *Perelandra.*" In *The Longing for a Form: Essays on the Fiction of C. S. Lewis.* Ed. by Peter J. Schakel. Kent, OH: Kent State UP, 1977. Pp. 73–90.

Kawano, Roland M. "C. S. Lewis and the Great Dance." *Christianity and Literature* 26 (Fall 1976): 20–38.

Kirkpatrick, John. "The Great Dance in *Perelandra.*" *CSL: The Bulletin of the New York C. S. Lewis Society* 7, iv: 1–6.

Merritt, James D. "She Pluck'd, She Did Eat." In *Future Females.* Ed. by Marleen Barr. Bowling Green, OH: Bowling Green State University Popular Press, 1981. Pp. 37–41.

Musacchio, George. "The Three Temptations of Perelandra's Queen." *Lamp-post* 1, no. 1 (1977): 3–5.

Myers, Doris T. "What Lewis Really Did to *The Time Machine* and *First Men in the Moon*." *Mythlore* 49 (Spring 1987): 47–50, 63.

Price, Stephen. "Freedom and Nature in Perelandra." *Mythlore* 29 (Autumn 1981): 38–40.

Rogers, Katherine A. "Augustinian Evil in C. S. Lewis's *Perelandra*." In *The Transcendent Adventure: Studies of Religion in Science Fiction/Fantasy*. Ed. by Robert Reilly. Westport, CT: Greenwood Press, 1985. Pp. 83–91.

Walker, Jeanne Murray. "Science Fiction: A Commentary on Itself as Lies." *Modern Language Studies* 8, no. 3 (1978): 29–37.

Warren, Eugene. "Venus Redeemed." *Orcrist*, no. 6 (Winter 1971–72): 14–16.

That Hideous Strength

REVIEWS

Bacon, Leonard. "Confusion Goes to College." *Saturday Review of Literature* 29 (25 May 1946): 13–14.

Beresford, J. D. "Five Novels." *Manchester Guardian* 24 Aug. 1945: 3.

Clare, Tullis. "New Novels." *Time and Tide* 26 (15 Sep. 1945): 777–78.

Collins, Leslie. "Tall Tales of Good vs. Evil." *Chicago Sun Book Week* 26 May 1946: sec. 5, p. 12.

Freemantle, Anne. "Truth, Terrors, Thrills." *New York Herald Tribune Weekly Book Review* 2 June 1946: sec. 7, p. 12.

Hamm, Victor M. "That Hideous Strength." *Thought* 21 (Sep. 1946): 545–47.

McSorley, Joseph. "New Books." *Catholic World* 163 (June 1946): 277–78.

Muir, Edwin. "New Novels." *Listener* 34 (6 Sep. 1945): 274.

"Myth Making." *Times Literary Supplement*, no. 2273 (25 Aug. 1945): 401.

Spencer, Theodore. "Symbols of Good and Bad in England." *New York Times Book Review* 7 July 1946: sec. 7, p. 10.

"Theological Thriller." *Time* 47 (10 June 1946): 52, 54.

CRITICAL INTERPRETATIONS

Callahan, Patrick J. "The Two Gardens in C. S. Lewis's *That Hideous Strength*." In *SF: The Other Side of Realism*. Ed. by T. D. Clareson. Bowling Green, OH: Bowling Green State University Popular Press, 1971. Pp. 147–56.

Collings, Michael. "Science and Scientism in C. S. Lewis's *That Hideous Strength*." In *Hard Science Fiction*. Ed. by George E. Slusser and Eric S. Rabkin. Carbondale: Southern Illinois UP, 1986. Pp. 131–40.

Hannay, Margaret. "Arthurian and Cosmic Myth in *That Hideous Strength*." *Mythlore* 2 (Autumn 1970): 7–9.

Lobdell, Jared C. "C. S. Lewis, Distributivist: His Economics As Seen in *That Hideous Strength*." *Orcrist*, no. 6 (Winter 1971–72): 20–21.

——— "Petty Curry: Salvation by a Taste for Tripe and Onions." *Orcrist*, no. 6 (Winter 1971–72): 11–13.

Lutton, Jeannette Hume. "Wasteland Myth in C. S. Lewis's *That Hideous Strength*." In *Forms of the Fantastic*. Ed. by Jan Hokenson and Howard Pearce. New York: Greenwood Press, 1986.

McClatchey, Joe. "The Affair of Jane's Dreams: Reading *That Hideous Strength* as Iconographic Art." In *The Taste of the Pineapple: Essays on C. S. Lewis as Reader, Critic, and Imaginative Writer*. Ed. by Bruce L. Edwards. Bowling Green, OH: Bowling Green State University Popular Press, 1988. Pp. 166–93.

Moorman, Charles. *Arthurian Triptych: Mythic Materials in Charles Williams, C. S. Lewis, and T. S. Eliot*. Berkeley: University of California Press, 1960.

Neuleib, Janice Witherspoon. "Comic Grotesques: The Means of Revelation in *Wise Blood* and *That Hideous Strength*." *Christianity and Literature* 30 (Summer 1981): 27–35.

Patterson, Nancy-Lou. "Anti-Babels: The Images of the Divine Centre in *That Hideous Strength*." In *Mythcon II Proceedings*. Ed. by Glen GoodKnight. Los Angeles: Mythopoeic Society, 1972. Pp. 6–11.

———. "Banquet at Belbury: Festival and Horror in *That Hideous Strength*." *Mythlore* 29 (Autumn 1981): 7–14, 42.

———. "Guardaci Ben: The Visionary Woman in C. S. Lewis' Chronicles of Narnia and *That Hideous Strength*." *Mythlore* 21, no. 3 (Summer 1979): 6–10, 21; no. 4 (Fall 1979): 20–24.

———. " 'Some Kind of Company': The Sacred Community in *That Hideous Strength*." *Mythlore* 47 (Autumn 1986): 9–19.

Purtill, Richard. "*That Hideous Strength:* A Double Story." In *The Longing for a Form: Essays on the Fiction of C. S. Lewis*. Ed. by Peter J. Schakel. Kent, OH: Kent State UP, 1977. Pp. 91–102.

Rawson, Ellen. "The Fisher King in *That Hideous Strength*." *Mythlore* 34 (Winter 1983): 30–33.

Reichenbach, Bruce R. "C. S. Lewis on the Desolation of Devalued Science." *Seven: An Anglo-American Literary Review* 4 (1983): 14–26.

Rose, Lois, and Stephen Rose. *The Shattered Ring: Science Fiction and the Quest for Meaning*. Richmond, VA: John Knox Press, 1970.

Schakel, Peter. "That 'Hideous Strength' in Lewis and Orwell." *Mythlore* 50 (Summer 1987): 36–40.

Spraycar, Rudy S. "C. S. Lewis's Mechanical Fiends in *That Hideous Strength*." In *The Mechanical God: Machines in Science Fiction*. Ed. by Thomas P. Dunn and Richard D. Erlich. Westport, CT: Greenwood Press, 1982. Pp. 19–26.

Starr, Nathan C. *King Arthur Today: The Arthurian Legend in English and American Literature, 1901–1953.* Gainesville: University of Florida Press, 1954.
Stewart, D. H. "What Lewis Really Did in *That Hideous Strength.*" *Modern Fiction Studies* 26 (1980): 248–54.
Stock, R. D. "The Tao and the Objective Room: A Pattern in C. S. Lewis's Novels." *Christian Scholar's Review* 9: 256–66.
Thompson, Raymond H. *The Return from Avalon: A Study in Arthurian Legend in Modern Fiction.* Westport, CT: Greenwood Press, 1985.
Timmerman, John H. "Logres and Britain: The Dialectic of C. S. Lewis's *That Hideous Strength.*" *CSL: The Bulletin of the New York C. S. Lewis Society* 9, no. 1: 108.

"The Dark Tower"

REVIEWS

Barnes, Julian. *New Republic* 15 Apr. 1977: 29.
Fowler, Alastair. *New Statesman* 25 Feb. 1977: 93.
Ryan, R. W. *Library Journal* 15 Apr. 1977: 102.

CRITICAL INTERPRETATIONS

Boenig, Robert E. "Lewis' Time Machine and His Trip to the Moon." *Mythlore* 24 (Summer 1980): 6–9.
Brady, Charles A. "Some Notes on C. S. Lewis's *The Dark Tower and Other Stories.*" *CSL: The Bulletin of the New York C. S. Lewis Society* 8, xi: 1–10.
Christopher, Joe R. "Touring *The Dark Tower.*" *CSL: The Bulletin of the New York C. S. Lewis Society* 9, vi: 9–13.
Hodgens, Richard. "Notes on C. S. Lewis's *The Dark Tower.*" *CSL: The Bulletin of the New York C. S. Lewis Society* 9, vi: 1–8.

INDEX

Note: Works by C. S. Lewis are listed by title; works by others appear under the name of the author.